TANGLED WINGS

Gatwick seen through green-tinted glasses

BRENDON SEWILL

The Aviation Environment Federation

ISBN 978-1-900211-01-7

Published in 2012 by
The Aviation Environment Federation
Broken Wharf House, 2 Broken Wharf
London. EC4V 3DT
T: 020 7248 2223
E: info@aef.org.uk
http://www.aef.org.uk

Printed by
Sherlock Printing
Unit 12, Redhill 23 Business Park
Holmethorpe Avenue, Redhill
Surrey. RH1 2GD
T: 01737 826595
E: mick.clark@sherlockprinting.co.uk
www.sherlockprinting.co.uk

Contents

Foreword
by Tim Johnson
Director of the Aviation Environment Federation

You don't have to search the media for long before you come across a story about aviation's impact on climate change or the latest proposal for a new runway to meet growing demand for air travel in the UK. Yet we need to remind ourselves that environmental issues surrounding civil aviation are not just a symptom of today's society: they have been around for decades. In fact, AEF's existence stems from a decision taken by communities affected by airfield and airport operations back in the 1970s to create a body that could represent their interests to policymakers at a national level. Many of these groups in fact tell a common tale: of fluctuating relationships with their respective aerodrome operators, of pressures for expansion, and of the difficulties involved in taking-on a well-resourced industry to get their voices heard. For some there have been periods of co-operation that benefited communities and the airport alike, but these are often interspersed with battles and lengthy public inquiries, and while some victories have been won along the way, it is rarely very long before the next phase of development plans are announced.

The history of the Surrey village of Charlwood, and its evolving relationship with Gatwick Airport, is in some ways typical, reflecting how attitudes and perceptions have changed with time, and how Government policy has both helped and hindered. But the Charlwood experience has also heralded some unique triumphs that make it stand apart. Obtaining a legal agreement preventing the construction of a second runway is an achievement unrivalled anywhere else in the UK. The upholding of this agreement, as well as a number of other concessions to the local community, has come about only through the persistence and dedication of the residents of Charlwood and, in particular, of the author of this book Brendon Sewill. Brendon has brought a wealth of experience, and a campaigning style characterised by both courtesy and humour that has benefited and inspired community and environmental organisations throughout the UK. Perhaps most notably, Brendon has introduced campaigning in this field to the idea that a successful argument needs to address economic as well as environmental impacts, and his publications on this topic have formed the backbone of many submissions to Government and had a tangible impact on public debate .

This book tells – with characteristic humour and insight – the story of how one village has stood up to its airport neighbour, and with its behind-the-scenes glimpses of the ins and outs of both local and national politics, it will be of interest to readers both with and without a personal connection to Charlwood.

Tim Johnson

Preface

Why am I interested in Gatwick? Just because I happen to live next door. And because I have done so since childhood. If I lived in Grimsby no doubt I would be writing an account of the fishing industry.

'If you don't like the airport,' the airline people always ask, 'why don't you move?' First, because every time there has been a runway threat our house could not be sold; every time the threat was seen off we felt no need to move. And second, because our village has been worth fighting for.

For millions of people, of course, Gatwick is a place to start happy holidays, a place to meet relatives and friends, a gateway to romantic destinations. For thousands it is a good place to work. None of that is denied: it is just a pity that aircraft make a great deal of noise; just a pity that the aircraft which use Gatwick are responsible for a growing amount of climate change damage; just a pity that the airport was put in a place where regular battles have had to be fought to prevent a new runway causing huge environmental damage.

This is a sort of autobiography and so I apologise if there is rather a lot about myself. But it is just about one part of my life. I wrote up my time in the Treasury in *British Economic Policy 1970-74*.[1]   As a somewhat premature attempt to justify the Keynesian full employment policies pursued by the Heath Government, it did not please Margaret Thatcher. More recently, I have written about my experience of running the Conservative Research Department

– at a time when it had a staff of seventy or so and a high academic reputation - in *Tory Policy-Making: the Conservative Research Department 1929-2009.*[2]   But this story is about the Gatwick side of my life.

Some Charlwood residents may be disappointed that it is not a proper history of the village, and may feel that too much emphasis is given to the airport. My mother wrote a history of the village up to 1950: in taking the history forward I have chosen to concentrate on the airport aspect because the repeated threats of airport expansion which would have left our village derelict, perhaps demolished, have been for Charlwood the key historical facts of the past sixty years.[3]

Some may be concerned that, by labelling Charlwood as a village over-shadowed by the airport, I am blighting their properties. Yet the threat from the airport is well known. My hope is that by setting out the reasons why runway proposals have been rejected so often in the past, this account can help to prevent them recurring.

Finally, some residents of nearby towns and villages may feel that there is too much about Charlwood. Yes, indeed, I plead guilty. Writing up the story of one village has a certain simplicity but of course thousands of people in scores of other villages and towns have opposed airport expansion. To make amends I am putting at the start of this book a list of all the 135 councils and environmental groups that have joined in the recent campaigns to preserve the character of the Surrey, Sussex and Kent countryside.

I would like to say a big thank you to all my Charlwood friends: Richard Bowling for the cover design; Charles Campen for drawing the maps; Colin Gates for his cartoons and photos; Jean Smith for the pen and ink sketches of Charlwood by her late husband, Barry; Irene Needham for the photo of the bluebells; and Leslie Thacker for the photos of Charlwood church.

Thanks are also acknowledged to Gatwick Airport Ltd for the photo of the earth bund; Osprey Publishing for the map of William's march; and Dave Thaxter for the photo of the helicopter over Gatwick.[4]   The photo of the North Terminal at Gatwick on the cover is by Martin Roell of Berlin.

Cait Hewitt, the erudite Deputy Director of AEF, made many sensible suggestions and gave me valuable encouragement by laughing at some of my stories.

Hilary, when she became my wife in 1959, had not realised that she was marrying an airport. When I told her that I was thinking of writing this book, she was fairly horrified and would have preferred that we could forget about Gatwick altogether. Nevertheless she has given me a huge amount of wise advice spiced with expert knowledge.

Brendon Sewill
November 2012

Councils and groups opposed to
a new Gatwick runway 1997 – 2010 [1]

Abinger Parish Council
Alfold Parish Council
Ardingly Parish Council
Ashurst Parish Council
Betchworth Parish Council
Betchworth and Buckland Society
Billingshurst Parish Council
Billingshurst Society
Bletchingley Parish Council
Buckland Parish Council
Brockham Green Village Society
Brockham Parish Council
Burstow Parish Council
Capel Parish Council
Charlwood Parish Council
Charlwood Society
Colgate Parish Council
Copthorne Village Association
Cowfold Parish Council
Cowden Parish Council
CPRE Surrey
CPRE Sussex
Cranleigh Parish Council
Crawley Down Residents
Crawley Friends of the Earth
Crawley & Horsham CPRE
Cuckfield Parish Council
Cuckfield Rural Parish Council
Danehill Parish Council
Dorking & District Preservation
Dorking District Naturalists
Dormansland Parish Council
Dunsfold Parish Council
East Grinstead Society
East Grinstead Town Council
East Sussex Transport 2000
Edenbridge & District Residents
Edenbridge Town Council
Esher Residents
Ewhurst Parish Council

Felbridge Parish Council
Forest & Riverside Neighbourhood
Forest Row Parish Council
Friends of Holmwood Common
Gatwick Anti-Noise Group
Godstone Parish Council
Guildford Borough Council
Hartfield Parish Council
Haslemere Society
Haven Preservation Society
Haywards Heath Society
Hever Parish Council
Hildenborough Parish Council
Hookwood Residents
Horley Local History Society
Horley Residents Association
Horley Town Council
Horley Anti-Runway Campaign
Holmwood Parish Council
Horne Parish Council
Horsham District Council
Horsham Society
Horsted Keynes Parish Council
Hurst Green Society
Hurstpierpoint Society
Ifield Village Association
Imberhorn Residents
Itchingfield Parish Council
Langton Green Rural Society
Leatherhead & District Countryside
Leigh (Kent) Parish Council
Leigh (Surrey) Parish Council
Leigh Residents
Limpsfield Parish Council
Lingfield & Dormansland Society
Lingfield Parish Council
Liphook Parish Council
Lynchmere Society
Meath Green Protection Society
Mid Sussex District Council

Mole Valley District Council
Newchapel and Lingfield Campaign
Newdigate Parish Council
Newdigate Society
North Horsham Parish Council
Norwood Hill Residents
Nutfield Conservation Society
Nutfield Parish Council
Nuthurst Parish Council
Ockley Parish Council
Ockley Society
One's Enough (Crawley)
Outwood Parish Council
Outwood Society
Oxted Parish Council
Penshurst Parish Council
Plane Facts (Cowden)
Quieter Skies (Godalming)
Reigate & Banstead Borough
Reigate Friends of the Earth
Reigate Society
Rowhook Amenity Society
Rudgwick Parish Council
Rudwick Preservation Society
Rusper Parish Council
Salfords & Sidlow Parish Council
Shipley Parish Council

Slinfold Parish Council
Slinfold Society
Southwater Parish Council
Speldhurst Parish Council
Surrey County Council
Surrey Wildlife Trust
Sussex Amenity Societies
Sussex Wildlife Trust
Tandridge District Council
Tandridge Friends of the Earth
Tandridge Parish Council
Trafalgar Neighbourhood Council
Turners Hill Parish Council
Twineham Parish Council
Uckfield Town Council
Warnham Society
Washington Parish Council
Waverley Borough Council
Wealden District Council
West Chiltington Parish Council
Westcott Village Association
West Hoathly Parish Council
West Humble Residents
Westerham Parish Council
West Sussex County Council
Woodmancote Parish Council
Woldingham Association
Worth Parish Council

The ill omen
1936 - 52

A man with wings jumped out of an aeroplane. The wings got tangled in his parachute.

'Don't look', said my mother, covering my eyes with her coat and thus thwarting my infant morbid curiosity.

That was the grand opening of Gatwick airport in June 1936. The aircraft were biplanes, the circular 'Beehive' terminal was ultra-modern, and the check-in time from train to plane was 20 minutes. The runways were grass, which was fortunate for the birdman: when he hit the ground he survived.

The press as usual ignored the good news – in this case a speech by the Secretary of State for Air[6] – and concentrated on the bad news. The tangled wings got the headlines, and were an ill omen.

The attempt to run a night mail service had to be abandoned after a crash. Another crash was caused, it was conjectured, by the radio officer getting his foot caught in the rudder controls. Indeed in those early days the aircraft equipment was rudimentary: on arriving over the South Coast the air crew had to lower their radio aerial and contact Croydon control tower using Morse code; on one flight a lady passenger had to surrender her hairpin to mend the radio fuse.[7]

The following winter Gatwick became a waterlogged bog. Jokes were made in the aeronautical press that water-lilies had been planted on the airfield; and that Gatwick was to be the new seaplane base.[8] British Airways moved out. In February 1937 the aerodrome was declared unserviceable.[9]

Despite the grass runways being reinforced with wire mesh, Gatwick had a less distinguished war record than Battle of Britain fighter bases such as Biggin Hill or Redhill. It was used mainly for reconnaissance flights, training and for aircraft maintenance.[10] Indeed it was still mainly a maintenance base in 1948, at the time of the Berlin airlift, when Leading Aircraftsman Sewill took time off from mending radar sets and hitched a lift to Gatwick on a clapped-out Dakota in order to get home in time for a days foxhunting.

Gatwick, situated on the borders of Surrey and Sussex, had been best known since 1891 for its racecourse where, during the first world war, the Grand National was held. The surrounding countryside was rural and agricultural, dotted with small historic villages. Charlwood, where my parents lived, was some two miles away and, although the aerodrome was in the parish, at first no one took it too seriously.

The name 'Charlwood' is said to be derived from 'Ceorl Wood', the wood that belonged to Saxon ceorls who were free men owing allegiance to no lord. Thus when my mother, with her friend Elizabeth Lane, wrote a history of the village they called it *The Free-men of Charlwood*. My own theory, which I will expound later, is that the churlish ceorls were in fact Saxon 'insurgents' rebelling against Norman rule. Their spirit lives on.

Only fourteen years after the battle of Hastings the Normans decided to build a church in Charlwood, of which the walls, arches and tower remain. In around 1280 John de Gatwyke added a new aisle to the church and sent his son off on a crusade. His home, Gatwick Manor, rebuilt in 1698, now lies under the North Terminal but some of his descendants still live in Charlwood. His son's ghost can be seen at midnight in Arrivals sadly looking for his lost escutcheon.

The village had a period of prosperity in the middle ages when the local woods produced charcoal used to forge iron. A number of small but substantial houses were built round the village green. Each had an open hall with a fire in the middle and the smoke going out through a hole in the roof. Five of these ancient houses were demolished when the new airport was built. Nevertheless twenty-eight small hall houses, dating from 1401 to 1500, survive today, more than in any other Surrey village.[11]

Richard Saunders, the local squire, foolishly died in 1480 when he was only thirty years old. His rich widow extended the de Gatwyke aisle, making a chantry chapel, with a magnificent screen, where prayers could be said daily to speed Richard's soul through purgatory. Belief in purgatory was abolished in the reformation seventy years later: it is to be hoped that Richard got to heaven before then. The medieval screen remains.

The village changed little until 1846 when an Enclosure Act was passed. Each house owner was allotted a part of the village green and – with a zeal which would have horrified council planners a century later – used it as a building plot. The result is that nowadays the village has a somewhat undistinguished Victorian centre while the old cottages - Charlwood has a remarkable total of over 80 listed buildings - are hidden away round the periphery.

In the 1950s the village was still essentially rural. Most men still worked on the farms. Many had been born in the village or in the neighbouring villages. They walked or cycled to work. Only about one in ten families had a car.[12] Carthorses were shod at the village smithy. The village butcher produced his own meat from the slaughterhouse next door to his shop. There were no main drains, and some houses still relied on their wells for drinking water. Many houses had no fixed bath, only an old tin tub.[13]

The roads were narrow with deeply rutted grass verges where cows or sheep were driven. The village was quiet. Dogs barked at distant farms, cocks crowed and one could hear the church clock a mile off. Indeed out hunting one could hear a pack of foxhounds, or a hunting horn, two miles away. Using one's ears, navigating one's own way across country on a trusted horse, jumping any obstacle that loomed up, that was real old-fashioned fox-hunting.

The nearest country town was Crawley, mainly distinguished by its coaching inn where in an earlier age an amorous Prince Regent, later George IV, driving his speedy phaeton, changed horses on the way to his mistress, Maria Fitzherbert, in Brighton. He would not recognise Crawley today: after the second world war it was designated as a 'New Town', and the population has grown to over 100,000.

There were few worries about Gatwick. Indeed in March 1949 it was announced in Parliament that Gatwick would be derequisi-tioned, meaning that it would not be developed as a major airport, and that Stansted would be developed as the diversionary airport for London. The Chief Executive of Crawley New Town was given an undertaking that Gatwick would never become a major airport with international scheduled services. Local people were blissfully unaware of the plots being hatched by Marcel Desoutter and Peter Masefield.

Desoutter had lost a leg in 1913, crashing an early Bleriot aircraft. But he designed his own artificial limb and kept his enthu-siasm for flying. In the 1930's he became manager of Gatwick, and during the war (surprising that people did not have more impor-tant things to do during the war) he commissioned consultants to draw up plans for how Gatwick could become a major international airport.

Masefield had first flown into Gatwick in 1932 in a Gipsy Moth biplane, and developed a life-long enthusiasm for the aero-drome. After the war he became head of long term planning at the Ministry of Civil Aviation and went on to become Chief Executive of British European Airways. While there he persuaded his old chums at the Ministry to reconsider the Desoutter plans.

Thus began at Gatwick the long tradition of secret co-opera-tion between the aviation industry and the civil servants that has so infuriated environmental campaigners over the years. Thus also began the revolving door between the industry and the civil service, most recently seen when, only two years after his retirement, the Permanent Secretary at the Department for Transport became the chairman of the Board of Gatwick Airport Ltd.[16]

Charlwood church

The fog deceit
1952 – 54

It came as a shock to the bucolic locals when, on 30 July 1952, the Minister of Civil Aviation, Alan Lennox-Boyd, announced that it was proposed to expand Gatwick airport. The announcement was deliberately low key. A written reply to a Parliamentary Question stated:

> *'It has now been decided to develop Gatwick as the southern alternative to London Airport and as a base for some scheduled services and other air transport activities.'* End of statement. It could hardly have been more low key.

The phrase ' alternative to London Airport' was well understood to mean an airport to which aircraft could be diverted when Heathrow was closed by fog – in those days the multitude of coal burning fires caused frequent 'pea-souper' fogs when one could not see to cross the road, let alone land an aircraft.

The decision to develop Gatwick had been taken by the Cabinet with the Chancellor of the Exchequer, 'Rab' Butler, in the chair and Lennox-Boyd in attendance for that item. The discussion was remarkably brief, as shown by the Cabinet Secretary's note:[17]

10   Gatwick Airport.

RAB. Agree: inevitable.   Put it into investment programme.

LB.   Will be staggered over many years.   Will discuss with Ty.   Agreed.

⌈ Exit LB.

'Agreed' – Gatwick was to be built, that was the decision taken. Exit Lennox-Boyd, undertaking to discuss with the Treasury how to fit the expenditure on building Gatwick into the investment programme. But when he published the plans three months later, they were not in the least low key or small scale. They showed a virtually new airport at Gatwick outside the boundary of the then existing aerodrome, with two parallel runways, and a shorter cross runway.[18] The northern runway, to be built first, pointed straight at Charlwood and would in effect have made the village uninhabitable.

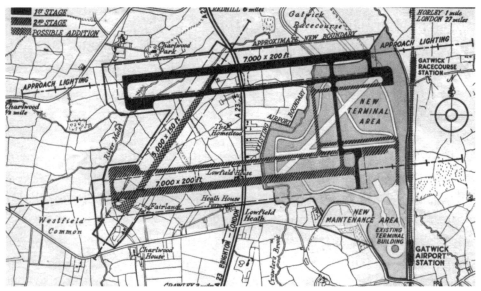

A Government plan for a virtually new airport was published in 1952. The northern runway, to be built first, pointed straight at Charlwood and would have made the village uninhabitable. The racecourse station was converted into the present station.

A Gatwick Protest Committee was formed. Meetings took place in an historic house, subsequently demolished, belonging to Jack Bowthorpe, a local businessman. My father, a rumbustious Master of Foxhounds with plenty of experience of running political campaigns, was a member, and so was I. Letters were written and the press was briefed. A public meeting, chaired by my mother, was held in Charlwood Parish Hall and attended by about 200 people. An indignant protest was sent to Ministers and to the local MPs.[19] Today that is standard practice for any environmental protest. But in 1952 we felt we were breaking new ground.

In one of our attempts to draw attention to the issues we erected large poster hoardings along the A23 (then the main London-Brighton Road, long before the M23 was built) designed as imitation road signs. 'Caution – road liable to disappear' one read, a reference to the fact that the main road would need to be diverted. Other posters were 'Round the bend' (silly to build such a large airport for comparatively few fog diversions); and 'Steep bill' (a reference to the high cost of building the new airport: £6 million, which seemed a lot of money in those days). I know what the posters said because they were subsequently used to construct our henhouse and are still there. Over the years the posters have not put the chickens off their lay; and at the time they appeared to make equally little impression on the Government.

Thirty years later, when the Cabinet papers were made public, we discovered that our campaign had been making more impact than we realised. At a Cabinet meeting held on 11 November 1952 the Minister of Transport was forced to admit that: 'in view of opposition to the proposed development of Gatwick Airport which was showing itself, especially among Government supporters, the Cabinet might wish to review their decision of 29th July.' A small committee of Ministers was appointed to review the decision, and to draft a White Paper to justify it. The octogenarian Prime Minister, Winston Churchill, muttered that, contrary to the opinions expressed by other Cabinet members 'he was by no means convinced that it would be right for the Government to reaffirm and make known for a second time their decision to develop Gatwick Airport before allowing local interests to express their views through some form of public enquiry.'[20]

Our campaign continued, mainly through a barrage of letters from the Protest Committee to the press, to Ministers and MPs. Distinguished experts were persuaded to give their views. Because my father had led the campaigns of the late 1940's opposing the nationalisation of road transport and other industries, and had done so in conjunction with the then Conservative Opposition, he was on first name terms with many members of the Government. The file is full of letters from Ministers addressed to him as 'Dear Roger', and from senior civil servants addressed, in the public school idiom of the day, to 'Dear Sewill'.

Nevertheless, when the Cabinet Committee reported back in July 1953, they recommended that the Gatwick plan should proceed but 'recognised that it would not be easy to satisfy public opinion as to the justification for this decision.'[21]

A Cabinet meeting on 21 July 1953, again chaired by 'Rab' Butler (because by then Churchill had had a stroke although that was being kept secret), confirmed the decision that Gatwick Airport should be developed as the 'main alternate' to London Airport.[22] 'The Cabinet Secretary's notes reveal the benefit of a classical education, the view of the committee being succinctly recorded as 'Aut Gatwick aut nihil.'

It was 'either Gatwick or nothing' because the choice of site for the new airport was dictated by criteria set by the Cabinet committee, and the criteria had been chosen so that no other site was suitable. The site had to be south of London, because that was the direction in which most people wanted to fly; had to have a good rail service to London; and had to fit into the then existing air traffic control system. Only Gatwick and nowhere else, so it was said, met these criteria.

The reason the Cabinet recognised that it would be difficult to justify the scheme was that the main public explanation given for needing a new airport was to provide a bad weather alternatve for Heathrow. Yet Gatwick was too close to Heathrow to have noticeably different weather, and the small number of diversions did not appear to justify the large size of the new airport.

The Government refused to admit what was obvious to everyone: that the new airport was intended to be the second main airport for London. It was not a good site for that purpose. With a hill to the west and the main railway line to the east, and with the towns of Horley and Crawley and the historic village of Charlwood close by, there was no room for future expansion.

A minor victory came when revised plans were published, and it was announced that the southern runway would be built first. To meet our warning that a plane might hit a train, the runway was moved half a mile further away from the railway. The A23 which previously was to have been diverted to the west, close to Charlwood, was instead to be diverted under the new airport terminal. Which is the reason why the Gatwick south terminal, unlike most other airport terminals in the world, has its arrivals and departures all on the same level.

The White Paper had been drafted, and the Cabinet Minutes record that it was decided to publish it in order to set out the 'arguments for proceeding with a project which may appear prima face to be open to such serious objections'.

Fog: that was what the White Paper concentrated on, stating: '*Gatwick will not be used intensively all the year round. Its principal purpose will be to receive aircraft diverted from London Airport when visibility is poor there and this purpose could not be achieved if too many regular services were based at Gatwick.*[23]'

Mark those words: they were the deceit from which the history of Gatwick follows.

In a pamphlet, *Gatwick airport: A Tragedy of Errors* (price sixpence), I attempted a detailed demolition of the Government's case, bringing together all the points made in correspondence during the previous year. The constraint imposed by the air traffic control system could be solved by drawing new lines in the

In 1953 the Government stated that Gatwick's main purpose would be to receive aircraft diverted from Heathrow because of fog.

sky. There were other aerodromes with better weather that could be used when Heathrow was fogbound. Poor visibility at Heathrow could be dealt with by the use of radar.

Not all my arguments proved correct. I put forward the idea that the fog could be dispersed at Heathrow by use of the wartime FIDO system which involved burning huge quantities of paraffin alongside the runway. The Clean Air Act was cheaper.

Some hapless civil servant had written that an advantage of Gatwick was that it would be possible to use the facilities of the existing aerodrome. When analysed these came down to the two narrow railway platforms of the former racecourse station and one cold water tap in the former grandstand.

The Ministry told us not to worry that the proposed northern runway would mean the end of the ancient village of Charlwood because 'it may never be built'. It was foolish, we retorted, for the Government to brush aside such concerns: better to plan a feasible two runway airport from the start.

Another public meeting, held in a works canteen at the old Gatwick airport on Guy Fawkes Night, became extremely raucous. The Minister of Transport, Alan Lennox Boyd, was due to attend to explain why the good weather at Gatwick made it a suitable alternative to Heathrow. His train was an hour late due to fog.

Fog caused other problems. The village postmaster, Mr Sidney Edney, doubled as reporter of village events for the local paper. Words did not come easily to him, and he had an old typewriter which was missing a key. After events such as public meetings, he always asked if I would be so kind as to write a piece for him but please avoid using the letter 'g'. Gatwick had to be 'the airport', and fog was 'bad visibility'.

Gatwick Manor

A poor choice of site
1954

The remarkable thing about the public inquiry, held in Horley in 1954, was that it lasted only 15 days, compared to nearly four years for the Heathrow Terminal 5 inquiry.[25] At the time we were satisfied that 15 days was sufficient to explore the issues which fell within the restricted terms of reference of the inquiry. Most of the discussion revolved around meteorological records showing whether Gatwick had more or less fog than Heathrow.

Despite Churchill's grumble, the Government had fixed the terms of reference to exclude any discussion of alternative sites. The Times printed a strong leader on this issue: *'The official argument for this costly and controversial project takes the form of repeating statements that have frequently been challenged. No alternative site is suitable; weather conditions at Gatwick are satisfactory... So much doubt has been thrown by responsible critics on these and other claims that a public inquiry, not merely limited to local considerations, should have been held before Gatwick was chosen.'*[26]

At the Public Inquiry the civil servants repeatedly emphasised that the principal purpose of the new airport was as a bad weather alternate for London Airport. The main opposition role was taken by Surrey County Council – at that time Gatwick was in

Surrey – and they listed the previous assurances that Gatwick would not be developed, and emphasised that the weather was not sufficiently different to that at Heathrow. Moreover, as their counsel pointed out: 'The site was too small for a modern airport ... [and] left little room for expansion, and its design and layout had been dictated by its confining smallness.'[27]

Giving evidence for the Gatwick Protest Committee, 'Slab' Kyle, a Canadian pilot who flew Constellations on transatlantic flights, and who lived in Charlwood (and whose grave lies beside the church lych gate), drew attention to the dangers posed by the high ground at Russ Hill.

In due course the Inspector found that the site was 'suitable' for the purpose proposed in the White Paper – but by implication not suitable as a major airport. He found 'considerable substance' in the criticism that the site was too small and could not be extended. Noise was *'a substantial point against the proposal.'* He also commented significantly that, *'As to whether it is the most suitable site which could be found, it is not, because of the limitation of the scope of the Inquiry, possible for me to express an opinion.'* [28]

The newly appointed Minister of Transport and Civil Aviation, John Boyd Carpenter pressed the Cabinet at a meeting on 7 September 1954 for permission to go ahead, adding 'the understandable local feeling against the proposal makes this a far from easy matter.' Winston Churchill, partially recovered from his stroke, was in the chair but was likely to have been more interested in several foreign affairs issues on the agenda. Harold Macmillan, who as Minister for Housing and Local Government had been responsible for the public inquiry, is recorded as commenting that: *'he would not oppose approval of Gatwick's development, although he greatly regretted the way in which the matter had been handled from the outset and had little doubt that the project would, in fact, cost more than the £6 millions estimated and might well prove in the end not to have been well founded from the point of view of our long-term civil aviation needs'.*[29]   How right he was.

A new White Paper announced the decision to go ahead. In it the explanation changed: fog became of secondary importance; instead the principal purpose was to provide '*a second main civil airport to serve London.*'[30]   Deceit was writ large.

In retrospect the site chosen was obviously too small for the role of the second main airport. It has never been possible to find an acceptable site for a second runway. So Gatwick remains as almost the sole major airport in the world operating with only one runway.[31]

After nearly sixty years, one has to ask 'what if'. What if the civil servants and Ministers had not tried to defuse the opposition by pretending that the main purpose was for fog diversions? What if it had been admitted that the real purpose was to provide a second main airport for London? What if the public inquiry had been allowed to consider whether another site would have been more suitable?

Even in those days thoughts were turning to the advantages of an airport in the Thames estuary where there would be fewer problems with noise and more space for future expansion. A well known London architect[32] submitted to the Protest Committee a fully worked out plan for an airport on the Isle of Sheppey with several runways (plus for good measure a seaplane base); the Chairman of the Sheppey Council planning committee wrote to the Times supporting the plan; and I recall driving over there one misty afternoon to inspect the site and sploshing about in the salt marshes.

The Gatwick Protest Committee had also submitted a memorandum – I still have a copy typed on long foolscap paper – to Harold Macmillan advocating, among other solutions, the construction of a new airport at Cliffe. '*It is an area of completely flat land, 26 miles from London, used only for grazing. No houses would have to be demolished, no trees felled, no roads diverted… Gatwick cannot be expanded should the need arise but there is room at Cliffe for three or four future Gatwicks.*'

Our proposal was rejected, mainly for the ephemeral reason that it did not fit in with the then pattern of air traffic flight paths. It had to wait until 2002 for the Government to put forward a fully worked out plan for a five runway airport at Cliffe as an alternative to new runways at Heathrow, Stansted or Gatwick. But by then the world had moved on: the airlines, especially British Airways, could not bear the thought of leaving Heathrow, and the sea birds at Cliffe had become too precious to upset.

Back in the 1950's we were all extremely cross about the fog deceit but the press soon lost interest. Like 'Plane Stupid' fifty years later, we felt a stunt was needed to draw attention to the Government's iniquity. When the advertisements for tenders to build the new Gatwick airport appeared in the press, my father and I applied, under the trade name of Sewill and Son, to build Gatwick Airport for £350,000. Our argument was that this sum was how much it had cost recently to build a landing strip at Lydd in Kent: if all that was required at Gatwick was a landing strip to handle fog diversions, a similar construction would be adequate. We were summoned to the Ministry: 'Are you serious?' Sir Humphrey asked. We had to admit that we were not.

The fog deceit implies that respectable civil servants and Government Ministers deliberately deceived the Cabinet and the public. That may sound far fetched but it is only necessary to read the autobiography of Harold Balfour, Under-Secretary of State for Air from 1938 to 1944, to discover that a similar deceit was practised when Heathrow was planned.

'Almost the last thing I did in the Air Ministry of any importance was to hi-jack for Civil Aviation the land on which London Airport stands under the noses of resistant Ministerial colleagues. If hi-jack is too strong a term I plead guilty to the lesser crime of deceiving a Cabinet Committee.' Balfour, knowing that acquiring the land for civil aviation in peacetime would involve 'complicated procedures', decided that *'our only hope lay*

in taking over [the land] under wartime powers,' and invented what he admitted was the fictitious need for a new bomber base. Thus Heathrow was never properly debated and never designed as a major civil airport, with the result that there is no space for a third runway and all arriving aircraft fly over central London.

At both Heathrow and Gatwick deceit has had a high cost. It has meant that London has finished up with five airports – Heathrow, Gatwick, Stansted, Luton and City – with six runways between them. None of the airports is now large enough to act as an effective hub for connecting flights. The French, by contrast, had the aeronautical good fortune to be defeated by Germany in 1870: after that, an area around Paris was kept free of houses so as to provide an open space for cannon fire. This wide open space has made a good site for Charles de Gaulle airport which has four parallel runways and is five times the area of Gatwick.

Laurel Cottage

Growing pains
1958 – 70

The new Gatwick opened in 1958 but at first there were few flights, and few diversions due to fog. The Clean Air Act 1956, one of the most effective Acts of Parliament ever passed, sorted out the fog.

Life in Charlwood continued much as before. Matins was said in church at 11.00 am every Sunday, as it had been since the first Queen Elizabeth; the 426 bus ran once every two hours to Horley; the Women's Institute made jam; the Mothers' Union held jumble sales; the British Legion paraded proudly on Armistice day; Mr Edney continued to report for the local paper without 'g's; the hunt continued to meet outside the Half Moon but decided not to draw Brockley Wood on the edge of the airport just in case fox and hounds might cross the runway at one of the rare moments when a plane was landing or taking off.

At around this time I decided to give up foxhunting and take up sailing. Sailing across the Channel in a 19 foot pre-war cutter with only a compass, a chart and a lead-line for navigation, and a usually defunct engine, provided plenty of good adventures. My maritime escapades and involvement in national politics wiped the airport off my mind for the next twenty years.

Russ Hill in Charlwood, which had featured large in the public inquiry, continued to feature large. In 1959 an aircraft crashed on the hill in fog, and a local farmer was surprised when a bloody figure stumbled into his house and turned out to be the Prime Minister of Turkey.[34] Since then fortunately there have been no crashes on the hill but there was one near escape in the 1980's when two engines out of four failed on an aircraft as it was taking off. A lady living on Russ Hill a mile and a half from the airport looked out of her bathroom window and was surprised to see the aircraft below her, between her house and nearby trees. A fearless passenger filmed the passing scenery: not surprisingly the film was somewhat shaky so nothing improper was revealed.

One is often asked what impact the airport has had on the village and on the surrounding area. Fortunately, as a result of our 1953 campaign, Charlwood does not lie under the flight path but to one side. The aircraft were unbearably noisy, especially in the 1970's and 1980's, but are now much quieter.

The biggest change has been the increase in car traffic, but that is something that affects most English villages. Curiously, the airport has preserved Charlwood. The high level of noise in the early years meant that no new housing was permitted. Thus, apart from some recent infilling, the village remains much as it was in 1960.

At a parish meeting in March 1965 a proposal for street lighting was defeated by 300 to 15.[35] So Charlwood voted decisively to remain rural, not to become a lit-up adjunct to the airport, and not to allow our brash new neighbour to destroy the historic character of the village. Like our neighbouring villages of Leigh, Newdigate, Betchworth and Rusper, we remain to this day in the dark, carry torches and can still, despite the glow from Gatwick, see a few stars.

When the airport was first built some of the richer gentry moved out. But they had to be very rich to do so, because houses in

Charlwood had lost half their value. There was no compensation. The Land Compensation Act passed in 1973 provided no retrospective relief: no compensation has ever been paid at Gatwick, except for the houses actually demolished when the airport was built.

Some of the big houses became hotels; others had a new type of owner. One day I bicycled down the village to call at a very grand house to ask the new owner if he would join a local village society. Sitting on an elegant sofa with his elegant wife, drinking elegant coffee, he was delighted to agree. The very next week the local paper reported that he had been charged with running a chain of South London brothels. I had to bicycle down again to cancel the invitation before he took up residence in the somewhat less elegant Wandsworth jail.

The proximity of the airport tends to attract some grubby characters. One can tell at a glance where some unsavoury activity is perhaps being conducted– just look for the leylandii trees!

Yet the experience of having to pull together once a decade to protect the village has resulted in a strong community spirit and has blossomed into a multiplicity of societies, clubs and activities. Many young couples say they chose to come to live in Charlwood because there is so much going on.

An airport consultative committee was set up in 1956, before the new airport opened. The chairman was appointed by airport owners, then the British Airports Authority. The members represented airlines, air passengers, local business, and local councils. They elected their own vice-chairman who in effect became the spokesman for local concerns. My mother was vice-chairman from 1956 to 1968; and my wife, Hilary, was vice-chairman from 1983 to 2008.

The fact that the Gatwick Airport Consultative Committee has been serviced by West Sussex County Council has given it a measure of independence and it has functioned better than similar committees at other airports that have been run by airport staff. The two Mrs Sewills, with their joint 37 years of environmental pressure, were able to achieve many improvements. Nevertheless the Consultative Committee, with its mixed membership, has never been able to take a firm line on key issues that run directly counter to the interest of the airport or the airlines, such as night flights or a new runway, and has never felt able to criticise the airport in public.

By the mid 1960's aircraft noise was getting far worse, and affecting a much wider area. The ear-piercing scream of the early jets, such as the Comet or the BAC111's, caused windows to rattle and brought conversation to a stop in Charlwood and Horley, and in many villages up to 15 miles from the airport.

The worsening environmental situation led to the setting up in 1965 of a new organisation, the Gatwick Anti Noise Executive (GANE). A petition to ban night jets attracted thousands of signatures and was presented to Parliament by the local MPs. In 1968 GANE transmogrified into the Gatwick Area Conservation Campaign (GACC), led by an energetic chairman, Doug Morris from Horley. Its membership mainly consisted of parish councils, and the five borough or district councils (but never Crawley) whose boundaries abut the airport. The councils have been remarkably loyal to GACC, and in recent years GACC has been able to claim a membership that includes around 60 councils and 40 local amenity groups.

Although I was not involved at the time, I have always assumed that it was the frustration with the lack of a single-minded environmental remit for the Gatwick Airport Consultative Committee which led to a choice of a title with the same initials. If the aim was to cause maximum confusion, the ploy was successful. Whatever environmental victories GACC may or may not have achieved, it eventually won the Battle of Acronym, with the Gatwick Airport Consultative Committee having to admit defeat and adopt the initials GATCOM.

Hilary's position as vice chairman of GATCOM for 25 years roughly coincided with my role as vice-chairman and then

St Michael's church lay at the centre of the village of Lowfield Heath, south of the airport. But in the 1970's aircraft noise made the village uninhabitable.

The village was demolished and now only the church remains among the warehouses and radar masts. The same could have happened to Charlwood.

A regular helicopter service between Gatwick and Heathrow was started in 1979. But it only carried ten passengers and annoyed thousands. The licence was withdrawn in 1983.

One of the conditions of granting permission for the North Terminal was the construction of large earth bunds, which have subsequently been raised, to protect Charlwood and Hookwood. This view is from the airport side.

The Lowfield Heath windmill was in a poor state of repair, and was at risk of being demolished to make way for airport warehouses.

In 1987, with work by many volunteers, the windmill was dismantled, moved to Charlwood, repaired, re-erected, and 'opened' by Princess Alexandra in 1990.

Edolphs Copse, threatened by runway proposals, has one of the finest displays of bluebells in the south of England.

The River Mole was diverted to allow space for airport expansion. Janis Kong (airport director), Laura Moffat (MP for Crawley), and Hilary Sewill (chairman Charlwood Parish Council) inspect the work at an early stage.

Aircraft have got quieter but are still extremely annoying.

The river diversion was done with sensitivity to provide an environmental improvement, with a pleasant footpath. The earth bunds built to protect Charlwood can be seen in the background.

FIGURE 4

DTp RUCATSE
Studies

**Gatwick
Runway Alignments
Studies**

SCALE 1 : 50000

One of a set of Illustrative Drawings
produced for the DTp in connection
with RUCATSE Studies.

The Department of Transport 'RUCATSE' Working Group in 1993 looked at three options for a new Gatwick runway, and chose the northern option.
That would have pointed straight at Horley, would have required a huge cutting through Stan Hill, and would have left Charlwood sandwiched
between the existing runway and the new one.

One anti-runway campaign got off to a false start when it turned into a heated dispute about the ownership of a red telephone box.

A civic service with an anti-runway theme was held in Charlwood church. From left Kenneth Baker MP, Hilary Sewill (Mole Valley council chairman), the Mole Valley chief executive, the Surrey county council chairman and the High Sheriff.

Church bells were rung and bonfires lit at 25 villages around the airport as a warning of impending danger (and to get press coverage). But an IRA attack on Heathrow stole the headlines.

Charlwood church has nationally important wall-paintings dated from c.1300. A project to restore the paintings culminated in an address by the Bishop of Southwark suggesting that it would be wicked to destroy them for the sake of expanding the airport.

An art historian created this reproduction of how the wall-paintings would have looked when originally painted. In this story a wicked lord makes a proposition to St Margaret, she refuses, is thrown into prison, is tempted by the devil in the form of a dragon, escapes but is finally condemned to death. But was she actually a fair-haired Saxon girl resisting the advances of a Norman knight?

In this painting three princes meet three skeletons who say to them: 'As you are, we were; as we are, you will be.' But was this subtle Saxon propaganda, hinting that the rich Norman knights would eventually get their comeuppance?

Charlwood's tendency to resist authority is demonstrated by the fact that the Rector of Charlwood was excommunicated by Archbishop Thomas Becket - four days before Becket was murdered in Canterbury cathedral.

It has been calculated that about 10,000 people are buried in Charlwood churchyard.

William The Conqueror's march on London

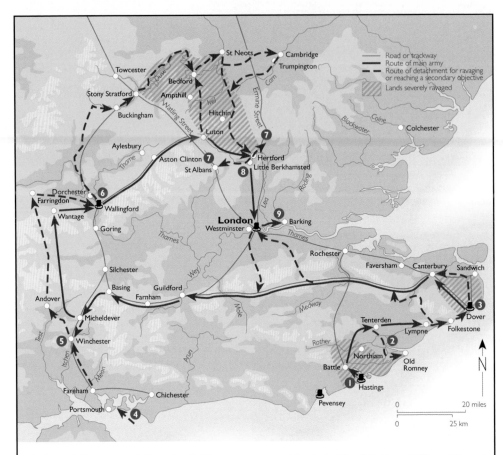

Charlwood's history may be linked to the Norman conquest. After the battle of Hastings, William followed a route which would have left many of King Harold's troops cut off in the weald. Perhaps, it is surmised, they formed a band of Saxon insurgents based on Charlwood.

1. Battle of Hastings 14 October 1066
2. Raid against Romney
3. Dover surrenders, castle constructed
4. Reinforcements arrive from Normandy late October
5. Winchester surrenders end October
6. Wallingford. Thames crossed and castle constructed
7. Ermine Street and Watling Street blocked to prevent reinforements reaching London
8. Early December. English leaders submit
9. William crowned at Westminster on Christmas Day, and retires to Barking.

chairman of GACC. It was a good partnership. Liaison meetings were held over early morning cups of tea in bed. Hilary was on good terms with the senior staff at the airport, and privy to a certain amount of confidential information, but no secrets were revealed. GACC functioned with an intelligent understanding of airport issues, and GATCOM was well informed on the concerns of local residents. We still count a number of former BAA staff among our friends.

As a result of being the leading environmentalist on GAT-COM, Hilary found herself during the 1980's and 1990's, along with Norman Meade who had a similar position at Stansted, on a Department of Transport technical committee dealing with aircraft noise and sleep research.[36] They were heavily outnumbered by the airlines but sometimes their logic prevailed, and in those cases their interventions enabled the civil servants to say 'Yes, Minister, but there is widespread feeling in the country that....'

The work of environmental groups around the world, and volunteers such as Hilary working through government departments, have put pressure on the aircraft manufacturers to produce quieter aircraft. It is always immensely satisfying to hear that manufacturers are designing new aircraft to meet stringent noise standards because of a fear that otherwise public pressure will not allow them to fly. One recent example is the giant Airbus380 with engines specifically designed to enable it to meet night flight rules at Heathrow.

If this account is mainly concerned with high profile runway issues, that should not obscure the immense amount of painstaking work done at Gatwick over the past fifty years to limit night flights, to steadily reduce the amount of noise permitted at night, to ban the noisiest types of aircraft, to impose noise limits and penalties on noisy take-offs, to attempt – unsuccessfully – to impose noise limits on arriving aircraft, to introduce the quieter system of continuous descent approaches, and to safeguard the countryside around the airport.

Rowley

Gatwick too small – where next?
1961 – 1974

It was soon realised that Gatwick was too small to cope with the growth in air travel, and that another airport would be needed. The ill omen of the tangled wings remained baleful. The search for a new airport has continued for many years, and is still continuing, rather like the Hundred Years War, with battles fought back and forth over the same ground. Kings may come, and Kings may go, but the war continues.

Between 1961 and 1964 an Interdepartmental Committee on the Third London Airport considered twelve possible sites. Three in the Thames estuary – Cliffe, Sheppey and Foulness – were rejected because of the cost of improving the surface access, because of the cost of building on marshy ground, and because of a military firing range at Shoeburyness.

Instead the Committee recommended Stansted. During the war the US Army Air Force had built a long runway there – now the main Stansted runway. The Interdepartmental Committee were, however, not content with one runway: they produced a plan for a four runway airport.

A vigorous opposition campaign was mounted, followed by a public inquiry with a much wider remit than the one at Gatwick.[37] Our moans about the terms of reference of the Gatwick inquiry – that they had prevented any discussion of alternative locations – had been heeded. The Inspector reported that he found that the

Stansted proposal would be 'a calamity for the neighbourhood' and should be rejected.

Nevertheless, a year later a White Paper gave the go-ahead for Stansted, not with four runways but with six![38]   By then a Labour Government with Harold Wilson as Prime Minister had gained office, proclaiming the need to harness 'the white heat of technology'. The aviation industry urged that a brand new airport was just what was needed to harness the white heat, and the Government suggested that, since they had inherited an economic crisis, building a new airport was essential to help the economy grow (a line that sounds all too familiar today). The House of Commons dutifully voted to proceed with the six runway airport. The House of Lords, however, with aristocratic wisdom threw the plan out.

To find a way forward, a Commission under Lord Justice Roskill was set up. They explored the merits of various sites, causing outrage and protest at each location. Their remit was to find a site for a new four runway airport: Gatwick, even with a second runway, was considered too small to be more than a stop-gap.[39] Finally they recommended a new four runway airport at Cublington, near Aylesbury.

The indignant people of Cublington mounted a strong campaign, ably assisted by Lady Hartwell, daughter of the formidable barrister and Lord Chancellor F. E. Smith, and wife of the proprietor of the Daily Telegraph; and by Evelyn de Rothschild whose stately home, Waddesdon, was nearby.[42]

A feature of the Roskill Commission was the first use of cost-benefit analysis, a system which has played a questionable part in all subsequent airport debates. It involves putting a notional value on the time saved by air passengers against the cost to the environment, but is not infallible: an article in the Sunday Times showed that, applying the same analysis, the maximum benefit would be achieved by locating the new airport in Hyde Park.

Meanwhile, in 1970, the British Airports Authority put in a

planning application to extend the Gatwick runway to 10,000 feet. At the same time they published proposals for a new runway at Gatwick, similar to the plan approved in the 1953 White Paper. As before, the northern runway would have made Charlwood unin- habitable.[40] The newly formed Charlwood Society held a meeting in the parish hall attended by over 300 people, reacting with anger to the proposals which would have meant the loss of 115 houses in Charlwood with many others in high noise or danger zones. Since the proposed runway would point straight at Russ Hill, it was noted that trees would need to be topped on the hill, not a procedure de- signed to increase confidence in airport safety.[41]

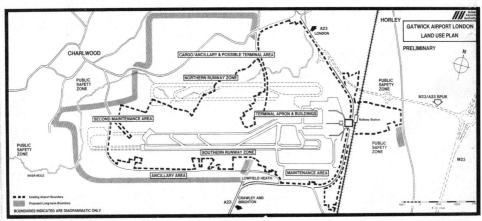

In 1970 the British Airports Authority produced a new plan, similar to the 1953 plan, for a two runway Gatwick. The resulting outcry helped persuade the Government to go for Maplin instead.

A public inquiry was held in Horley. It opened in St Francis' Hall on 17 November 1970, and was unusual in one way: on the first day the Inspector died. Strong opposition was mounted by GACC led by Doug Morris, and by the Surrey and West Sussex County Councils. GACC gained strong support from all the surrounding area. Horley, a town with a population of around 20,000, would have been seriously affected. So would Newdigate, Capel, Ockley, Copthorne and Lingfield. Gordon Lee-Steere, squire of Ockley (and now vice Lord Lieutenant of Surrey), as GACC membership sec- retary, helped to raise £20,000; a QC was instructed, and professional advice was commissioned on noise, aviation and economics. Although the Inquiry was formally restricted to discussing the runway lengthening, the strength of opposition implied even greater opposition to the new runway.

Permission for the Gatwick runway extension was granted, but the strength of public opposition at Gatwick, and at Cublington, and at Stansted, made it abundantly clear that further development of inland airports was not acceptable. A solution was at hand: one of the Roskill members, Colin Buchanan, Professor of Transport at Imperial College, and at that time Britain's most illustrious planner, had put in a minority report in favour of a new airport to be built on the sands off Foulness in Essex.

The new Prime Minister, Edward Heath, coming into office in June 1970, adopted the Foulness idea with gusto. Airport planning was something he understood. After the war, he had joined the civil service and had been posted to a junior job in the Ministry of Civil Aviation's Long Range Planning Department. His boss was the arch-exponent of Gatwick, Peter Masefield. There is no record that Heath was involved in decisions about Gatwick but, as he recalled in his autobiography: *'I sat on numerous committees, including one overseeing the building and development of the new airport at Heathrow. Every time I arrive at Heathrow I shudder to think that I was in any way involved in the creation of that monstrosity.'*[43]

I worked closely with Ted Heath from 1965 to 1970 but never once had a discussion about Gatwick or indeed about airport policy. He was a man to whom casual conversation did not come easily, an intensely reserved man who kept each part of his life – politics, music and sailing – in watertight compartments and firmly shut up any attempt by anyone from one compartment to try to chat about his activities in a different one. Airport planning was one such compartment: he did not welcome views from anyone he did not consider a distinguished expert.

On becoming Prime Minister he took immediate and decisive action to promote Foulness. A Cabinet committee was set up, chaired by the Home Secretary, Reggie Maudling. In due course Maudling presented a paper to the Cabinet, proposing that the third London Airport should be built at Foulness: 'There is little time to spare' he told his colleagues, 'if we are to prevent expansion of Gatwick and maximum use of Heathrow and other airports, with all the public opposition that would provoke because of the resulting increase in noise nuisance.'

Renamed more hygienically 'Maplin', the plan for the new four runway airport was announced in April 1971. The project, due to open in 1980, would have included not just a major airport, but also a deep-water harbour, a high-speed rail link, new motorways and a new town. 'For the first time a government taking a major national decision has given pride of place to the environment' claimed Heath.

Maplin was designed to take the pressure off Heathrow and Gatwick. Indeed, in writing to give permission for the Gatwick runway extension, the Department of the Environment added *'The decision to construct an airport at Foulness.... has enabled the Government to abandon the safeguarding of the line of a second runway at Gatwick .... when the new airport is operational it will be used to relieve Gatwick and so enable air traffic noise to be reduced.'*[45] Much rejoicing in Charlwood. I regret to say that we did not show much concern for the (then rare, now common) Brent geese on the Foulness sands.

Rapid progress was made: planning permission was granted and in 1973 construction started; a gravel 'trial bank' 300 metres long was erected to see if an airport could withstand the North Sea storms. The bank is still there, still withstanding the storms, but the airport plan soon sank.

The British Airports Authority (then publicly owned) had opposed the project from the start, seeing it as a rival, likely to take traffic away from Heathrow and Gatwick. British Airways hated the idea of leaving Heathrow where they had a cosy monopoly of slots.   Practical problems caused the Maplin opening date to be postponed to 1982. Right wing Tory MPs who disliked Heath (the antipathy was mutual) began to grumble about the cost. It emerged that large numbers of houses would need to be demolished in order to construct the new motorway into London. Opposition was strengthened when the British Airports Authority suggested publicly that the existing London airports could cope with the forecast traffic 'almost indefinitely.'[46]

One of the first decisions of the new Labour Government in 1974, in the dark days of the coal strike and oil crisis, was to cancel Maplin. Three weeks after the election, the new Trade Secretary, Peter Shore, announced a review; and brought his con-clusions to the Cabinet on 12 July. Air traffic forecasts were lower and no need was seen for a new runway for London before 1990. Maplin would cost £600 million whereas expanding Heathrow and Gatwick would cost only £300 million. 'From the point of view of noise and safety,' Shore told Harold Wilson and his Cabinet, *'a decision to abandon Maplin will be bitterly opposed by those who live around the existing four London area airports, and around those regional airports which might take traffic diverted from the South East.'* And in a sentence which rings very true today, he added: *'To abandon Maplin now entails risks about future airport capacity ...'.*[47]

Maplin was the biggest public project, and the most far sighted airport development, ever conceived in Britain. These days it is unfashionable to find a good word to say for Ted Heath but he deserves credit for Maplin at least. The costs involved, even allowing for inflation, were tiny compared to the costs now quoted of £50 billion for a new Thames Estuary airport. The possibility of a further postponement was apparently never discussed. The decision set the pattern for London's airports, and meant that the wings of airport policy remained firmly tangled. Instead of one big airport we would have a ring of small airports. By the 21st century it had become clear that each was too small to act as the hub that the aviation industry, and many in the City of London, so desired.

More Charlwood battles
1972 – 1980

Meanwhile at Charlwood we had our own local battle. As part of a nationwide reform of local government (the Local Government Act 1972) Charlwood, Horley and Gatwick airport were designated to move from Surrey into West Sussex.[48]   At a public meeting an elderly resident hoped that it might be warmer if we went into Sussex because it would be further south, but this was generally felt to be optimistic. Going into Sussex would have meant Charlwood becoming submerged in Crawley. As a Labour-dominated New Town, Crawley was in favour of airport expansion, wanted more industry, had little care for the countryside or for preserving the heritage, and was already casting covetous eyes on the green fields around the airport for future housing sites. Horley had similar fears that their schools would suffer if merged with Crawley.

A demonstration by 1,500 residents disrupted traffic on the main London to Brighton road at the proposed boundary.[49] Charlwood and Horley residents marched through London to the House of Commons, carrying a petition in the form of an unrolled roll of toilet paper (in those days it was painfully strong and hard) with a signature on each sheet. The Government had other things to worry about. In the middle of the coal miners' strike and the three day week, the Charlwood and Horley Act 1974, keeping us in Surrey, was passed. It was touch and go: Royal Assent was granted on the last day before Parliament was dissolved – the day Ted Heath opened his unsuccessful election campaign. As The Times reported: *'83 bills are lost but three vital measures pass all stages today.'* [50]

Thus, thanks in part to the loo roll, Charlwood stayed in Surrey, and became part of a newly formed District Council called by the Wind in the Willows name of 'Mole Valley'. Horley stayed in Surrey and became part of Reigate Borough. A new parish of Salfords and Sidlow was created.

The airport went into West Sussex. The Charlwood to Horley road became the boundary between Surrey and Sussex, the boundary of the green belt and the boundary of the airport. Because Surrey and Mole Valley have subsequently applied ultra-strict planning policies, Gatwick is still bordered by open countryside on its northern and western sides. Unlike Heathrow, the airport has not become surrounded by warehouses, factories, hotels and other airport tat. Charlwood village has not become dominated by airport parking or by B&Bs.

Lowfield Heath was a small village on the southern edge of the airport, originally part of Charlwood parish. But noise had made life there intolerable, and in 1973 the whole village was zoned for industrial development. Home owners sold up and moved out. All the houses in the centre of the village were demolished and replaced by warehouses. Nothing was left except a windmill, of which more anon, and the church which still stands forlornly on the edge of the runway, an appropriate religious symbol seen by millions of air passengers at the moment they fasten their seat belts and pray. An affectionate and nostalgic history of the demolished village, *Lowfield Heath Remembered,* was later written by the Charlwood historian, Jean Shelley. It was a grim warning of what might happen to Charlwood were a second runway ever to be built.

The cancellation of Maplin led to strong pressure to expand Gatwick. A large extension of the terminal (now the South Terminal), including a new entrance, new multi-storey car parks and the Hilton hotel was designed to take the capacity of the terminal from

5 million passengers a year to 16 million. A taxiway to the north of the main runway was converted into an 'emergency runway'. It is too close to the main runway to be used at the same time without the aircraft wings getting tangled, but is available if there is an 'incident' on the main runway or when the main runway is being re-surfaced. It causes much terminological confusion. The press frequently refer to the need for a second runway – but there are already two runways.

The British Airports Authority also wanted a new terminal (now the North Terminal) to enable the airport to handle 25 million passengers. Local Councils were, however, still annoyed by the fog deceit and were not prepared to trust either the airport or the Government. They feared that, if planning permission were given for the new terminal, the next step would be a demand for a new runway. 'Oh, no', the British Airports Authority (BAA) said, 'we would never, never, want another runway.'

Fortunately the West Sussex County Council had a far-sighted planning officer, Peter Bryant (later to become the chairman of the airport consultative committee) and a wily lawyer, Michael Holdsworth. 'OK', they said, 'if you never want another runway, sign here on this legal agreement.' Thus was born the legal agreement, signed on 14 August 1979, that prohibited any new runway for forty years.

The reason BAA were prepared to sign was that the only place they could have put the new terminal within the airport boundary was where it is now, but that was bang in the line of the second runway as proposed in 1953 and 1970. Moreover, by then BAA had concluded that there was no suitable site for a second runway at Gatwick, and were pinning all their hopes on a large new two-runway airport at Stansted.

Holdsworth's skilful drafting has withstood every attempt by governments and by the aviation industry to find a legal loophole. Why was it forty years? Holdsworth told me that he had suggested: 'In perpetuity.' BAA retorted: '20 years.' So they split the difference.

Subsequently a similar situation arose at Heathrow. BAA wanted permission to build Terminal 5. *'Does this mean that you will next ask for a new runway?'* they were asked. *'Never'*, said BAA emphasising the point with a banner headline in their tame newspaper: *'Third Runway Ruled Out. BAA has said repeatedly – there will not be a third runway.'*[51] The T5 Inquiry dragged on for nearly four years. Six months after it concluded, BAA asked for a new runway.

At Gatwick we were fortunate that our legal agreement was based on the 1949 Planning Act, and was unbreakable. More modern agreements based on section 106 of the 1991 Planning Act can be appealed against. Since it is the government that ultimately decides appeals, and since governments are usually in favour of airport expansion, section 106 agreements provide no cast-iron guarantee.

The 1979 runway agreement brought quiet rejoicing in Charlwood, but it was overshadowed by the immediate need to oppose the new terminal and the plans for a new aircraft maintenance area on the Charlwood side of the airport. It was not so much the terminal building to which we objected, more the inexorable increase in the size of the airport.

The North Terminal Inquiry opened in January 1980 and ran for six months. GACC, the Charlwood Parish Council and the Charlwood Society were jointly represented by Philip Otten QC. Because we had very little money, he agreed to forego the services of a supporting solicitor so long as we found someone to brief him. This task fell mainly on my wife Hilary who was by now chairman of the Parish Council. It involved attending the Inquiry every day, intervening where necessary, assembling a large volume of papers in neat order in cardboard boxes, and travelling up to the Middle Temple to brief Otten before he appeared. The experience taught us a lot about how to present evidence, and how to influence the outcome of an Inquiry.

Neil Matthewson from Rusper, then chairman of GACC, opened our case. Three local MPs and twenty others also gave evidence on behalf of GACC. A further 25 people from Charlwood, including the Rector, gave evidence for the parish council: each spoke on the character of the village and their fear that it might become overshadowed by this ever-growing monster of an airport. Their evidence provides a good social study of the village as it was then.[53]

Towards the end of the inquiry there was a visit to the site where the plans showed a new maintenance area. One of the rules of site visits is that, to ensure fair play, an Inspector must at all times be accompanied by representatives of both sides. The Inspector, John Newey, plunged into the bog, brambles and wild roses of Brockley Wood. Hilary plunged with him. All the rest, in their smart blue suits and polished black shoes, held back. Hilary has always attributed the success of our case to the personal relationship she established in Brockley Wood.

The result of the Inquiry was that, although permission was given to go ahead with the new terminal, it was on condition that huge earth bunds, 13 metres high, were constructed to protect Hookwood, the part of Charlwood parish to the north of the airport. Centuries ahead, long after Gatwick is no more, the earth banks will remain, like Offa's Dyke. Permission was refused for the new maintenance area, and Brockley Wood remains standing to this day. Until that time BAA used to boast that they had never lost a planning appeal, but they had counted without the wild roses.

Windmills and helicopters
1980 - 1989

Living next to an airport has had some advantages.

The 900th anniversary of the building of Charlwood church fell in 1980, and it was decided to hold a festival to raise funds to prop up one of the church walls. What made Charlwood different from other villages we asked ourselves: a wealth of medieval houses and proximity to an airport. We managed to persuade the owners of the old houses to lodge American visitors for a week; and to persuade British Caledonian – whose head of public affairs lived in the village – to advertise the festival in Houston, and to put on a special flight.

The festival week, organised with élan by Charlwood resident Nick Hague, was a huge success. There was a son et lumière show depicting the history of the church, a meet of the foxhounds, a cocktail party in a moated manor house, and a barn dance in champion motor-cyclist Barry Sheene's barn. A special festival ale was brewed. Princess Alexandra came to a children's fancy dress party. The culmination of the week was a medieval jousting tournament at Edolphs Farm. About 40,000 people attended - or tried to attend since the roads were jammed solid in all directions. The knights jousted, a British Caledonian helicopter hovered anachronistically overhead, a brewers' dray drawn by four large carthorses took fright and bolted, one of the blue-rinsed American ladies was mown down. Despite that mishap, many of the American visitors remain to this day good friends of their Charlwood hosts; and the concept of inviting American visitors to stay in villages was taken up by the Church of England and rolled out (to use more modern jargon) to parishes across the country.

Another benefit of living next to an airport came from the demolished village of Lowfield Heath, on the southern side of the airport. Back in 1926 a benevolent philanthropist, Thomas Mason, had given the Charlwood Parish Council an acre of land beside the Brighton road to be kept in trust as a recreation ground. When the village was demolished the land became overgrown with brambles.

One of the parish councillors had an acquaintance who worked for a property company. The property company offered the unbelievably huge sum of £201,000. For the council whose annual income was under £3,000 that was riches beyond all possible dreams. Indeed one pure-minded member of the council felt it would be wrong to be so greedy.

Against the wishes of a majority of the council, Hilary, who had by now become council chairman, insisted on seeking competitive tenders. Eventually the land was sold on 5 January 1982, to Duracell, a local Crawley firm, for £490,000.[54]

This vast financial windfall for Charlwood caused a good deal of heated debate. The majority of councillors felt the money should remain in the control of the Parish Council. The Charity Commission advised that it should be set up as a separate charity. Hilary agreed with the Charity Commission, and resigned as chairman.

A public meeting was arranged for 4 March 1982. Around 200 people squeezed into the Parish Hall for what the rector, David Clark, described in the parish magazine as "the most gloriously entertaining night out the community has enjoyed for many a long year."[55]   The parish council sat on the platform and presented their plans of how they intended to spend the money. Hilary was presented with a bouquet of flowers to thank her for her work as Chairman.

A voice from the back of the hall asked if Mrs Sewill could explain why she had resigned. She did and, as the rector recorded, "the meeting loudly and decisively backed the stand Mrs Sewill had taken." Even the official minutes of the meeting record "Cries from the floor of 'trustees out' and disgraceful'.

After more furious debate someone shouted "stand up all who want a vote", and the whole hall stood up. A resolution that the Charity Commission proposals be adopted was passed over-whelmingly. As the rector wrote: "Those who chose TV that night made a grave mistake."

After those somewhat traumatic birth pains, Hilary became chairman of the trust, and remained chairman for 25 years. In 1999 the Thomas Alexander Mason Trust merged with another local charity, the John Bristow Charity which had been set up in 1637 to provide education for poor Charlwood children. The trust now has a capital of around £2 million, and an annual income of around £80,000, all of which has to be spent in the parish of Charlwood.

The trust fund has made possible many good works such as the renovation of the church, the parish hall and the sports pavilion, improvements at Charlwood school, the build-ing of a new hall in Hookwood, and the provision of two children's play areas, not to mention grants to those in need and to assist young people with their education. More generally the effect has been to keep the village in good nick and prevent it becoming a run down airport slum as might so easily have happened.

The fund has also made possible the purchase by the Wood-land Trust of large areas of woodland, now with full public access. These included Glovers Wood, a Site of Special Scientific Interest, and Edolphs Copse. John Edolph is recorded as living in Charl-wood in 1314, and has left his name both to Edolphs Farm, where the jousting took place, and to the copse – a 65 acre ancient wood-land where in late April the sea of bluebells is a mind-blowing experience. Edolphs Copse was to play a leading role in subsequent runway battles.

In 1985 there was a threat that part of the wood might be converted into a large gipsy encampment. From my youth I remember the gipsies camped at the top of Stan Hill, with their horses tethered on the grass near the caravan, and the smell of wood smoke from the camp fire as I rode home in the dusk after a long day's fox-hunting. In their ancient nomadic philosophy they had strict rules to keep the inside of their caravans spotlessly clean, but to throw the rubbish out and move on. By the 1970's, however, all this was changing. The horse-drawn caravans were replaced by motor vans, the road side verges were narrower, the jobs on the farms had dried up. Motorway construction required large groups of workers. The public were fed up with mess, no longer biodegradable but plastic, broken prams and rusty bicycles. National policy was to herd the gipsies into council provided sites. Paved with concrete and surrounded by wire mesh and barbed wire, these sites closely resembled concentration camps. By the 1980's it had become Government policy to compel county councils to pro-vide an adequate number of sites for the gipsy population in their area. Some of the sites got a poor reputation. There was one, for example, not far away, in Outwood where 30 or so gipsy families lived in squalor, and terrorised the neighbourhood. No one could go in without a police escort, and on one occasion 120 police had to go in wearing riot gear to make 12 arrests.[56]

Surrey County Council picked on a site at the top of Stan Hill for a new gipsy site for 16 (or more) gipsy families. The 12 acre site, originally part of Edolphs Copse, had been used by the District Council for some years as a tip for raw sewage, but since gipsies were held in low regard no one worried too much about that. The consent of Mole Valley District Council was needed before the plan could proceed. The council had 41 members but only one, Hilary, from Charlwood. All the rest were inclined to think that it would be best to stuff the gipsies down in Charlwood, in the far south of the District, rather than risk getting them in their own patch. So we started at odds of 40 to 1 against.

A meeting was held in the Parish Hall at which a great many insults were hurled at gipsies, and they were accused of committing every possible petty crime, and a good many unpetty. The rector was so upset that he organised his own counter meeting in the church.

Praying was not sufficient, action was needed. Edolphs Copse, adjacent on two sides to the proposed gipsy site, was up for sale. We contacted the regional manager of the Woodland Trust, who by chance was our daughter. The Thomas Alexander Mason Trust agreed to put up the money. Christopher Lowe, a high-powered accountant, visited the local bank manager and insisted he cancel the bank's acceptance of a lower offer. The wood was bought and our local MP and Cabinet Minister, Kenneth Baker, emphasised the beauty spot message when he attended an opening ceremony.

The date for a decision by the District Council was approaching. About twenty or thirty sites had been surveyed, and the recommendation was likely to be Stan Hill. The voting still looked like 40 to 1 in favour.

We came up with what we called 'the small sites policy'. Instead of having one large site, why not have eight small sites each with only two or three gipsy families? This would have a number of advantages. Each site would be much less intimidating. Council officers could go in without the need for a police escort. Each family would become known individuals instead of part of a large amorphous group. Any petty crime could more easily be dealt with. Experience with existing small sites, such as the one at Povey Cross in Charlwood, showed that the gipsies took much greater care of a site for which they had personal responsibility, and thus there was less litter and mess. Politically small sites might be more acceptable as they would spread the burden more fairly and avoid the huge public opposition to the big sites.

How to convince the 40 Councillors? In British politics, national or local, there is a well founded tradition to discount an argument put forward by anyone who has a perceived interest in the matter. By contrast there is a tendency to accept as gospel any argument put forward by consultants. We needed consultants, but there was only 10 days to go, and we had no funds to pay them. Topher Crump, a surveyor, who lived on Stan Hill, provided the solution. His firm had a subsidiary company called CNP Management. We persuaded them to write up in suitably erudite language the merits of the small sites policy. Topher produced professional looking maps. The CNP report, bound in smart glossy covers, was distributed to all Councillors.

On the night the gallery was packed. Hilary, who was by now vice-chairman of the Planning Committee, made a powerful speech setting out the wrongness of spoiling the beautiful Stan Hill woodland, and commending the CNP report. The result was an overwhelming majority against Stan Hill and in favour of small sites.[58]

Over the succeeding years the small sites policy was implemented, and has proved an outstanding success. Hilary became chairman of the Mole Valley gipsy committee, responsible for the welfare of the gipsy families and became friends with several. Fear and lawlessness became things of the past. The gipsies looked after their sites with pride. Whether as a result of our example or not I do not know, a similar policy has been adopted in many parts of England. Topher and I never owned up that it was we who had written the CNP report.

The annihilation of Lowfield Heath had left a decrepit windmill, also threatened with demolition to make space for more airport warehouses. Built around 1740, it was a post mill - the oldest type of mill where the whole upper body turned around a central post to enable the sails to face the wind. A committee, subsequently a charity, was formed. I found myself chairman, but the moving spirit and technical expert was Peter James, a young man from Crawley who knew all that could be known about windmills. Crawley Council declined to compel the owners to repair it. The only way to save it was to move it. We looked at a site on the top of Russ Hill and consulted the Civil Aviation Authority. Because it would have been under the flight path, they said that the sails would need to be lit at night. Revolving red lights would have been pretty. Another site, however, at the bottom of the hill, proved more suitable.

With the aid of substantial grants from the Thomas Alexander Mason Trust and from the Heritage Lottery Fund, and with an immense amount of work by volunteers, the windmill was carefully dismantled, repaired, re-erected and restored to full working order. Princess Alexandra made a return visit to 'open' the restored windmill in 1990. If you fly out of Gatwick to the west, as 75 per cent of planes do, the windmill is clearly visible to starboard.

When we had been looking for a place to repair the windmill we found a large empty barn in Edolphs Copse. Permission to borrow it was given without hesitation by the Woodland Trust manager. The barn had previously been owned by a pilot with Uganda Airlines who had got planning permission in order to keep pigs. But there were no pigs, there never had been any pigs, and when we came to clear out the barn we found it half full of tins of Coca-Cola waiting for export to Uganda.

The River Mole (so called because it sometimes flows underground near Box Hill) had to be diverted when the airport was first built. Kilmanham Bridge, where the women of Charlwood are said to have slaughtered the Danes in AD 850, lies under the runway. When the runway was extended, the river had to be diverted again. Finally, in 1999 it had to be diverted yet again round the outside boundary of the airport. This time we – GACC and Mole Valley Council - managed to attach a condition to the planning permission that the new river should be properly landscaped. The airport director, Janis Kong, threw her heart into the project, working enthusiastically with the local councillor, Hilary. The result, an attractive winding river full of rosebay willow herb, bulrushes and wildlife, with a pleasant riverside walk open to the public, and well used by local dog walkers, can be counted as an advantage brought by the airport.

A regular helicopter service from Gatwick to Heathrow had started in 1979. Although only flying once an hour there and back, its regular route and distinctive blade slap caused a disproportionate amount of annoyance. An application by British Caledonian to continue the service came up in 1983, and was opposed by Surrey County Council and GACC. Unlike a usual planning application, this was to renew the licence to fly the route, and was heard by the Civil Aviation Authority. For several weeks I took time off from my office in Lombard Street to attend and give evidence at the CAA offices in Kingsway.

The County Council did an opinion poll of people under the route, and we worked out that about 150,000 people were annoyed by each flight – and each flight carried only ten passengers once an hour. The M25 had recently opened, and we were able to show that a bus service running every 15 minutes would be more efficient. The CAA politely noted what we said but proceeded to grant the licence on the grounds that their terms of reference did not allow them to give any weight to environmental issues. The helicopter chief pilot commiserated with me and gave me a tie with a picture of a helicopter on it.

The decision had to be confirmed by the Transport Minister, David Mitchell (owner, incidentally of the Fleet Street wine bar immortalised by Rumpole, and father of Andrew Mitchell, of 'you pleb' fame). It had been assumed that this was a mere formality but GACC wrote to him summarising our case, and pointing out that, unlike the CAA, he was permitted to take environmental considerations into account. The licence was rescinded, and no regular helicopter services have operated in the London area since then. I still have the tie.

As Gatwick grew ever busier there was increasing pressure for industrial and commercial development. Developers cast covetous eyes on all the green fields to the north of the airport, around Charlwood, which were designated as green belt where virtually no development was permitted. Throughout the 1980's and 90's there was a constant battle to resist planning applications, and then to fight the inevitable appeals.

An investment company applied in 1983 for permission to build a high technology business park on 88 acres of green fields north of the airport. It was strongly opposed by Surrey County Council and by Mole Valley District Council; Hilary presented the Parish Council case, and permission was refused. Two years later another application, to build a 400 bedroom hotel, 300 houses and a research centre on the same land was seen off. A comparatively minor point mentioned in the case against the first application was that it would have meant destroying about fifty fine oak trees. At the time of the second application it was discovered that the owner of the land had attempted to kill all the trees by cutting a ring of bark around each.

Those were the two key planning decisions that have preserved the open country to the north of the airport. BAA were so pleased with the success of this policy, together with the landscaped River Mole diversion, that they advertised Gatwick in the national press as 'the airport in the country.' Unfortunately this attractive farmland looks an ideal site for a new runway.

To the south of the airport, West Sussex County Council and Crawley Borough had a policy of preserving a strip of countryside, called somewhat pompously 'The Strategic Gap', between the airport and Crawley with the aim of preventing the town and the airport from coalescing. Sound planning. But it has created an open space into which a runway could be squeezed, and indeed it is this land that, since 2003, has been safeguarded for a potential new Gatwick runway.

Because around Gatwick there was so much money at stake, the developers could afford to pay for the best advocates. Debating with high-powered QCs sharpened our wits. When Tesco wanted to build a supermarket in Hookwood, they employed a barrister called Roy Van de Meer, later to become better known as the Inspector at the Heathrow Terminal 5 Inquiry. They got their supermarket but Hookwood got some surplus land which was landscaped into a children's play area, the Withey.

There are some people who take great joy, and derive great profit, in cocking a snook at the planning authorities. Peter Vallance was one such. He turned old turkey sheds on the Gatwick side of Charlwood into industrial units, eventually getting retrospective permission. He bought a bright red aeroplane and parked it at the entrance to his industrial units. Planning permission was refused. The aeroplane stayed put. Indeed he acquired 15 other aircraft of the 1940 - 1960 era, and parked them in the field behind his works. The planning authority said it was green belt and that the planes must go. Vallance held open days for visitors, recruited hundreds of aviation enthusiasts to sign petitions, and applied for permission to build a large hangar with a taxiway leading off Gatwick airport. Those with suspicious minds saw a plot to expand the airport by stealth. Permission for the hangar was refused, and it has not been built. The planners, backed up by the Parish Council, imposed enforcement orders to remove the aircraft. Vallance appealed. The independent Inspector backed the council. But the Council was not prepared to face the adverse national publicity of sending in the bulldozers to break up this 'unique collection of historic aircraft'. Stalemate continued for twelve years. Another planning application, for an even bigger hangar, was submitted in 2011. Again it was refused. Again Vallance appealed. Again an Inspector backed the council, saying that, however valuable the aircraft collection, it was more important to preserve the green belt, especially in the gap between the airport and Charlwood. So still the aircraft stay put.

Off-airport car parking has proved a profitable crop for local farmers. Even at £1 a day per car it yields far more than growing wheat or keeping sheep. As soon as the planners catch up with the cars in one field, it is easy to move them to another. Cowboy car parkers also have had a field day. One firm advertised 'valet parking', met unsuspecting victims at the airport, and dumped their cars on the side of public roads. Or made good use of them – one owner of a rather smart car came back to find it full of confetti.

Another problem has been the 'established use' provision in the planning laws. If you can conduct a business use for four years without challenge, or build and occupy a house for ten years, you are automatically eligible for planning permission. One local farm concealed their large off-airport car park behind straw bales, and after four years admitted that they had deceived the planners but got their permission. A house was built hidden inside a barn. It is vexing when people make money by deception. A simple amendment to the law – to prevent established use being claimed if council tax had not been paid – would solve the problem.

By and large, however, the planning system, operated by councillors and dedicated council officers who care about the environment, has succeeded remarkably well in preserving the countryside around Gatwick.

During Margaret Thatcher's reign Kenneth Baker was Secretary of State for everything in turn, finishing up as Conservative Party Chairman. Geoffrey Howe, Member for East Surrey, was Chancellor and then Foreign Secretary. Both were personal friends of mine from my previous political existence. Both were firmly opposed to a second runway, not because of my influence but because that was the view of the majority of their constituents. With such friends at court we did not have too much to fear.

The 1980 Gatwick North Terminal Inquiry was followed by a public inquiry into the BAA proposal to develop Stansted. It was hard fought by the residents of Hertfordshire and Essex, led by the doughty Susan Forsyth. To placate them the Inspector recommended that 'an unequivocal assurance' should be given that there would never be a second runway at Stansted.

The 1985 Airports Policy White Paper gave the go-ahead for Stansted and 'unreservedly accepted' the unequivocal assurance. That did not deter the British Airports Authority who proceeded to build an airport terminal obviously designed to be at the centre of a two runway airport. The white paper also ruled out a new runway at Gatwick, stating: *'The Government believes that the provision of a second runway would have unacceptable environmental implications ... the village of Charlwood would be destroyed...'*

By 1989 the Select Committee on Transport was again recommending a second runway at Gatwick. Knowing that in those days the Committee consisted of backbench MPs who were transport enthusiasts but who had failed to get a Ministerial post, we did not take the threat too seriously. It seemed a good opportunity to train up a new team of local campaigners. So we got together an inexperienced committee, and they decided the first thing to do was to raise some funds. An event was organised at a local country hotel with the special attraction of women's mud wrestling which, however sexy, seemed somewhat unconnected to influencing government aviation policy.

The real crunch, however, came with the raffle for a red telephone box. In the excitement of the mud wrestling, only ten out of 300 tickets were sold. So the next day the hotel owner generously stumped up for the remaining 290, and installed the telephone box outside his front door. Then one of the ten asked when the draw was to be held. 300 counterfoils were put in a hat, and by a massive stroke of misfortune, one of the original ten drew lucky. She demanded her telephone box. The hotel owner had cemented it to the ground and maintained he had bought it. Both sides were offered large sums of money but refused to budge. Both nearly went to court. All the energies of the anti-runway committee were absorbed in sorting out the telephone box imbroglio. Almost unnoticed, the Select Committee report was forgotten.

Down the Gatwick Gorge
1990 – 1994

It was therefore with some surprise that in January 1990 I received an invitation from the Secretary of State for Transport to serve on the new RUCATSE Working Group. The curious acronym stood for RUnway CApacity in The South East, and the task, yet again, was to find the best place to build a new runway which, according to the forecasts made by the (pro-aviation) Civil Aviation Authority, would be needed by 2005.

The study was led by the Transport Department (in those days it was The Department for Environment, Transport and the Regions – DETR). There were about forty members, half civil servants, a good many representatives from airlines and airports, plus two from each of four airport environmental groups. Neil Matthewson and I represented GACC, Norman Meade led for Stansted, Evelyn Attlee led for Heathrow, and Moira Logan spoke for the Airfields Environment Federation assisted by a young man called Tim Johnson.[61] We became firm friends.

The three airport groups, Heathrow, Gatwick and Stansted, immediately got together and agreed a 'non aggression pact': we would each fight our own corner but would not advocate putting the runway in each other's patch, and would not criticise each other's case. Previously airport campaigners had pressed for other airports to be expanded - anywhere but not in my backyard. In the 1980's the Surrey and West Sussex County Councils had set up a well-funded organisation to lobby for a new runway at Stansted.[62] Uttlesford District Council at Stansted retaliated by putting in a planning application for a new terminal at Heathrow. But our non-aggression pact stopped that and started a trend for all anti-airport groups to co-operate. We had learnt that only the airlines benefited when we fought each other; and learnt that one could not proclaim environmental purity while wishing environmental harm to others. Apart from one lapse which I will describe later, that principle has held firm during all the airport battles of the past twenty years.

The full RUCATSE Working Group met every two months but in between there were meetings of the noise and environment subgroups. It was all conducted in secret, which was sensible in order not to blight dozens of different places. The first year was spent looking at alternative airports in the South East to see if any of them could provide relief for Heathrow and Gatwick. I remember especially the debate about the former US air base at Greenham Common, near Newbury. The man from the Ministry of Defence was wheeled in. 'It would be impossible to convert the air base to civil use,' he explained patiently, 'because there is a treaty with the Soviet Union which allows Russian inspectors to visit the base once a year to check that no nuclear weapons were stored there.' When some of us in the environmental squad expressed doubt as to whether that was a sufficient reason to rule it out for a civil airport, he came up with another reason: 'There is a group of women anti-nuclear protesters camped outside. If it was turned into a civil airport it would be very bad publicity to have them camped outside the main entrance.' That too did not seem totally convincing.

A firm of civil engineers put forward the idea of building a new airport on an artificial island in the Thames Estuary. They called it Marinair. The advantages were that few people would be affected by noise or pollution, and there was unlimited space for future expansion. The terminal was to be onshore near Tilbury at a place called 'Mucking' which seemed as unappetising as 'Foulness'. Passengers were to be conveyed by high-speed bullet trains to the door of their aircraft. The civil servants were sceptical but invited the engineers, and their Japanese financial backers, to give a presentation to the RUCATSE Working Group. Instead of a constructive discussion on how the idea might be made to work, the airlines set about rubbishing it. The main objection I recall was that passengers' baggage would get lost on the transit from the terminal to the aircraft.

The real flaw was that Marinair would only be financially viable if the number of flights at Heathrow, Gatwick and Stansted were limited. As had been the case with Maplin twenty years previously, British Airways hated the idea of being forced to move some flights from Heathrow, and BAA (by now privatised) hated the idea that they might not be given ownership of the new airport.

Thus the Transport Department ruled out Greenham Common, ruled out Marinair, and ruled out everywhere else: the new runway must be at Heathrow, or Gatwick, or Stansted.

The civil servants and their aviation friends got together and decided against a southern runway at Gatwick, mainly because it would be inefficient – aircraft from the two existing terminals would have to cross the existing runway to get to the new runway. Instead they came up with a proposal for a new runway to the north of Gatwick. The plan was horrific. The runway would have run from Gildings Barn in Partridge Lane, Newdigate to The Black Horse pub in Hookwood, and would have pointed straight at Horley. An enormous cutting over a kilometre wide and 50 metres deep would be excavated through Stan Hill. All the open fields between Charlwood and Horley would be turned into aircraft parking areas around a new terminal, with a new motorway link north of Horley.

The boundaries of the new airport were skilfully drawn to

leave Charlwood still standing but isolated between the two runways. When I asked at RUCATSE how people would get to the village, the answer from the civil servants was 'Through tunnels.' When I pointed out that no one in their right minds would wish to live in such circumstances, the answer was *'Perhaps the houses could be used as temporary accommodation for transient airport workers.'*

$$\sum_{tt}\sum_{i=2010}^{2040} \frac{(SC_{B,tt,i} + SC_{O,tt,i}) * (Ta_{O,tt,i} - Ta_{B,tt,i})}{2 * (1.06)^{i-2010}}$$

Campaigning against a new runway can be challenging. This formula, to prove the case for the new Gatwick runway, was produced by the Department 24 hours before the final meeting of the RUCATSE Working Group.

The civil servants kept the calculation of 'passenger benefits' until the last meeting of RUCATSE, when there was no time to analyse and challenge them. That looked like a deliberate ploy, remembering how the cost-benefit analysis of the Roskill Commission had come unstuck when closely examined. It was the beginning of an era when phoney 'passenger benefits' were calculated by the Transport Department statisticians to justify overblown runway plans. Next time round we were able to demonstrate why the calculations were dubious.

The report of RUCATSE was published in July 1993, at the same time as the Twyford Down road protests, and very inconveniently just three days before our daughter's wedding. The eight of us from the environmental campaign groups wrote a minority report in which we argued that more weight should have been given to environmental issues; that the damage caused by a new runway at Heathrow, Gatwick or Stansted should rule these locations out; and that the possibility that several more runways might be required in future meant that an estuarial site, such as Marinair, should be given more constructive consideration.

Our minority report was not newsworthy and made no impact. We had to wait sixteen years until these views were adopted by the Coalition Government and the Mayor of London.

Although the main report was carefully expressed in neutral terms, just giving the pro's and con's of each site, the arguments looked distinctly weighted in favour of the Gatwick runway. A new full-length runway at Heathrow was virtually ruled out because it would mean demolishing 3,300 houses, and the RUCATSE terms of reference curiously did not permit consideration of a shorter runway. Nor did it seem to make much sense to build a new runway at Stansted when none of the airlines wanted to go there.

The report, in its drab civil service prose, was grim reading for Charlwood: *'The major off-site impact relates to the historic village of Charlwood which ... would lie between the ends of the two runways. We considered that the location of the village in relation to the airport would severely compromise its habitability, and creates (sic) human and physical problems. Charlwood has 1,146 residents in 462 dwellings, with a conservation area comprising 42 listed buildings and a Norman church (Grade 1). Road access to Horley and to smaller settlements to the north would be severed probably necessitating the construction of road tunnels.'*

In case anyone did not take the point, the report added; *'Charlwood might well suffer the same fate as the former neighbouring village of Lowfield Heath on the airport's southern boundary where airport uses have now taken over completely.'* [64]

At that stage there was no government announcement on whether Heathrow, Gatwick or Stansted was the preferred site, and the golden rule of all campaigns is to influence a decision before it is taken. Trying to reverse a government policy after it has been announced, with Ministers having to lose face and bow to public pressure, is far more difficult. So there was no time to lose.

A public meeting was organised in Charlwood, and because of the numbers (and because it made better television) was transferred from the parish hall to the church. Over 350 people crammed in, standing room only. We explained the plans while a BBC television crew filmed from the pulpit. The Rector was asked if he got as many people to his Sunday services. *'No'*, he replied, *'but I would if the Almighty was so foolish as to threaten to demolish this village!'*

Yet of course a second runway would have affected a far wider area. It was not just a 'landing strip' as some of the press called it: it would have doubled the size of Gatwick with double the number of planes and double the noise.[65]   During the following year I addressed 38 other town and village meetings with audiences between 20 and 400, and members of our committee did other meetings. All voted unanimous opposition. One of the issues that caused most concern was the need to build tens of thousands of new houses for airport workers, which would have led to the destruction of much well loved Sussex countryside.

GACC, and many local councils and groups, prepared detailed responses to the consultation. Over 5,000 letters were sent to the Department of the Environment. But we realised that polite responses would not be sufficient: to influence the Government we had to make a bigger fuss.

The local authorities got together and decided to appoint a liaison officer - Liz Curtis who had cut her environmental teeth organising volunteers for the BTCV. She and Julie Lowe, chairman of the Charlwood Society, and I met once or twice a week to coordinate a joint campaign. The campaign slogan we chose was *'Down the Gatwick Gorge: no [run]/ way'* – the gorge being the proposed cutting through Stan Hill. The message was designed to warn the public of the potential safety hazards, but in practice it proved somewhat too abstruse and never really caught on.

Liz organised a council tax petition in which 4,500 people asked to have their council tax valuation reduced because the value of their property had been blighted. This was a novel type of petition which we hoped would be newsworthy, but it failed to make the national press, and had a downside. Several months later the

District Valuation Officer decided that the petition represented 4,500 applications for tax reassessments, and asked GACC whether we wished to undertake the work involved in representing all those who had signed.

Graham Capel from Newdigate constructed a 'noise van' which toured the area making a roar like an aircraft taking off. Every Saturday Graham and Julie took the van – when it did not break down – to a town centre, Horley, Redhill, Reigate, Dorking, Cranleigh, Horsham, and Crawley, and to many villages, and handed out thousands of leaflets describing the fate that would befall the area.

Julie organised 25 villages all to ring their church bells and light bonfires one evening in February to warn of impending danger in the time honoured fashion. Unfortunately the evening was cold and wet, and by pure bad luck, at the same time the IRA launched a mortar attack on Heathrow. The police, jittery that our protest was an attack on Gatwick, went round putting out all the bonfires and threatening to arrest the bedraggled villagers standing around them. In the way of the world, the three IRA men who broke the law got all the headlines in the national press, and our damp law-abiding protest got none.

Liz arranged for the local authorities to send out leaflets to everyone on their electoral rolls – over 100,000 leaflets. Hilary, who was that year Chairman of Mole Valley Council, led a delegation of the chairmen of all the neighbouring County and District councils to see the Aviation Minister. Allies were recruited, including the Woodland Trust (whose wood, Edolphs Copse, would have disappeared down the runway cutting), and SPAB, the Society for the Protection of Ancient Buildings, who did a survey of all the historic buildings due to be destroyed or made uninhabitable by the runway. The Charlwood Parish Council dreamt up a 'photo petition'. Photographs of all 500 houses in Charlwood, with a sentence from every householder saying why they did not want their house or village destroyed, were bound into a book and delivered to

Before the airport, Gatwick used to be most famous for its racecourse. The Grand National was run here during the first world war.

St Nicholas' church, Charlwood, was built only 14 years after the battle of Hastings, and is listed grade 1 - of national importance. It is about a mile from the end of the runway but fortunately not under the flight path.

A flying club started at Gatwick in 1930. Hunts Green Farm was used as the clubhouse.

When Gatwick opened as an airport in 1936 the 'Beehive' terminal was ultra-modern. But the grass runways soon turned into a bog, and most airlines left.

How much longer, wonder Charlwood men (l. to r.) Arthur Standing, Raymond Thirkell, Tom Wickens and Jack Shephard, will they be able to worship in the Saxon church and drink in the centuries-old pub behind them?

In 1952 the people of Charlwood were astonished to hear of plans for a large new airport, with the runway pointing straight at the village.

19

Lowfield Park, where the Gatwick Protest Committee met from 1952 to 1954. This was one of several historic houses demolished when the airport was built in 1956.

A meeting of the Gatwick Protest Committee. The chairman, Wilfred Watson, is at the head of the table with the author, looking young and earnest, on his left.

Prime Minister Winston Churchill thought it wrong to decide to go ahead with the controversial Gatwick plan before a public inquiry.

The Crawley Courier
The Biggest and Best Local Newspaper

FRIDAY, SEPTEMBER 4, 1953 — Postage: Inland 1½d. Abroad 1½d. — THREEPENCE

ROADSIDE SLOGAN BATTLE AGAINST GATWICK

Let them prosecute, says Mr. Sewill

"FIGHT LIKE HELL" AGAINST GATWICK

A start on the town centre

THOSE HUGE RUNWAYS WOULD BE A WAR BASE
New town in a target area — what local people think

Large placards were erected along the London-Brighton main road to draw attention to the many doubtful aspects of the proposals. The Mr Sewill who courted prosecution was the author's father.

Harold Macmillan greatly regretted the way in which the Gatwick proposal had been handled, and 'had little doubt that the project might well prove in the end not to have been well founded from the point of view of our long-term civil aviation needs.'

Larkins Farm was another of the medieval houses demolished when the airport was built. But over 80 listed buildings remain in Charlwood.

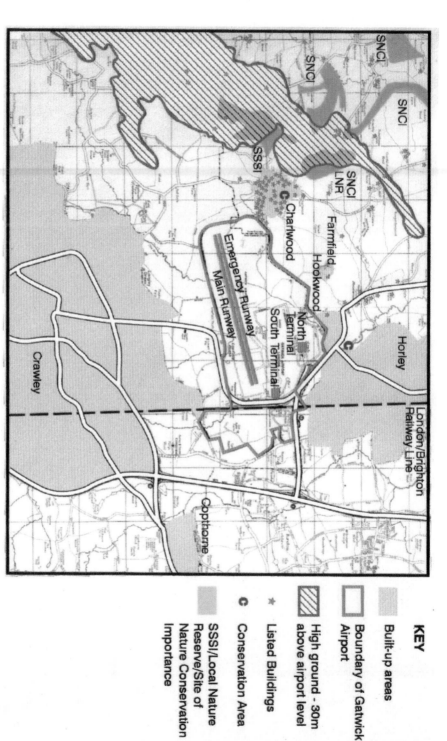

This map demonstrates how Gatwick is confined between the towns of Horley and Crawley and the medieval village of Charlwood, with high ground to the west. The map was produced by Mole Valley Council in 1993, and only shows listed buildings in Mole Valley. The emergency runway (built in the 1970's) and the main runway are too close together to be used at the same time.

KEY

- Built-up areas
- Boundary of Gatwick Airport
- High ground - 30m above airport level
- Listed Buildings *
- Conservation Area **C**
- SSSI/Local Nature Reserve/Site of Nature Conservation Importance

Gordon Lee Steere played a major role in the early days of GACC, collecting funds to fight the 1970 public inquiry.

Looking down on Gatwick from the top of Russ Hill. This ridge of hills - Russ Hill, Stan Hill, Norwood Hill - is one reason why a northern runway has never been built.

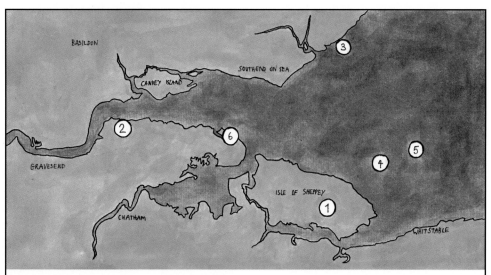

The Gatwick Protest Committee suggested that it would be more sensible to build a new airport in the Thames Estuary, where fewer people would be affected by noise and pollution, and where there would be unlimited space for expansion. Since then many others have had the same idea.

1. Sheppey. Proposed by the Gatwick Protest Committee 1954, and supported by local people at Sheppey.

2. Cliffe. Proposed by the Gatwick Protest Committee 1954, and by the Department for Transport 2003.

3. Maplin. Planning permission granted 1972. Construction about to start 1974.

4. Marinair. Considered by the Transport Department 1993.

5. 'Boris Island'. Proposed by Boris Johnson, Mayor of London. 2010

6. Hoo. New airport proposed by the architect Sir Norman Foster. 2011.

DON'T WORRY OLD CHAP, AS SOON AS THE RUNWAY BECOMES OBSOLETE IN TEN YEARS TIME WE'LL BUILD YOU A BRAND NEW ONE........

Local artist and song-writer Colin Gates, whose ancestors have lived in Charlwood since before 1200, drew this cartoon for one of the anti-runway campaigns.

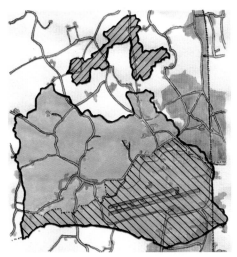

Prime Minister Edward Heath's decision to build a new four runway airport in the Thames Estuary at Maplin was far sighted. The decision in 1974 to cancel the project has left London without an airport large enough to compete with Paris, Amsterdam or Frankfurt.

Charlwood parish (green) originally included Gatwick. Legislation was passed in 1972 to move Charlwood and Horley into West Sussex (with the detached northern part going into a new parish of Salfords and Sidlow). A special Act of Parliament in 1974 moved Charlwood and Horley back into Surrey - but Gatwick (the southern shaded area above) stayed in West Sussex.

Downing Street.

The chairman of the District Council had the traditional annual duty of arranging a civic church service. Hilary decided to hold it in Charlwood church. All the local dignitaries attended, including the High Sheriff in velvet and lace. Kenneth Baker read the lesson (on the Judgment of Solomon with, we assumed, the hidden meaning that governments had to make difficult decisions but should come down of the side of those who felt most love for the area). The Rector preached on the wickedness of breaking legal agreements. Determination to defeat the runway was reinforced.

It was extremely difficult to get press coverage for opposition to a project which was only one of three options put forward in a report and where no Government decision had been taken. It is ironic that after a government decision has been announced, the press and television are keen to report protests – when it is too late. Only one of our events in the RUCATSE campaign made it into the national press, and that took two years to come to fruition.

Charlwood church has some fine wall paintings dating from around 1300. They had been covered with whitewash during the Reformation, rediscovered in the 1850's, and needed restoration. We raised £10,000 and Canterbury Cathedral provided an expert restorer. With an eye to a potential press story, an art historian was recruited to produce a painting, now hanging at the back of the church, reconstructing what the murals would have looked like when first painted. When the restoration was complete the Bishop of Southwark was invited to a ceremony. We managed to get the architectural correspondent of the Daily Telegraph interested. Jon Lloyd, Mole Valley head of planning, sat on a tombstone with a strange modern device the size of a brick called a mobile phone relaying the Bishop's words to the Telegraph. The painting of the murals, and our case against the runway, made it into the newspaper.

As a climax to the campaign, Liz organised an anti-runway festival to be held in a large field at the top of Stan Hill, on the line of the proposed runway. Celebrities were invited, events arranged, local musicians composed anti-runway songs, knights in armour were hired, publicity went out all over Surrey and Sussex. It might have been a forerunner to the Climate Camp at Heathrow. Then for three days it rained, the field was waterlogged and on the day the heavens wept buckets. With sadness, only partially alleviated by the fact that we had insured against bad weather, we decided to cancel.

The most effective weapon in our campaign proved to be an unexpected one. A year before the RUCATSE report was published, when I knew what was coming but was bound to secrecy, I took the precaution of encouraging the Charlwood Society to produce an illustrated picture book on Charlwood. The Horley camera club took photos. Sir Matthew Farrer agreed to write a foreword. Matthew is an old friend of mine, and we have both lived in Charlwood for most of our lives. His father was solicitor to the Royal family and dealt with the fall out from the abdication crisis in 1936. Matthew followed in his footsteps, coping with Royal divorces. He would never have dreamt of getting mixed up in any political campaign but signing a foreword to a village picture book with no mention of runways seemed uncontroversial.

By a curious historical quirk another Charlwood resident, Thomas Saunders, grandson of the young man who went to purgatory in around 1480, became solicitor to Henry VIII, arranging his divorce from Anne of Cleves. He too must have been careful to keep out of politics as he went on to hold high office under Edward, Mary and Elizabeth.

Portrait of Charlwood was a pretty booklet and copies were distributed far and wide in support of our plea that the village should not be made derelict. What we had not anticipated, and would never have had the presumption to suggest, was that a number of elderly Charlwood ladies sent copies to Prince Charles, Princess Alexandra (who had a soft spot for Charlwood from her two recent visits) and other members of the Royal family. The Royals, perhaps recognising Matthew, forwarded the picture book to the Transport Secretary with suitable expressions of concern. Powerful lobbying!

In due course the Government announced its decision. The main finding was that the airlines and the CAA had exaggerated the urgency of the need for a new runway, and that it would be not in fact be needed until around 2013. With a ten year lead period for construction, the decision could be postponed until about 2003.

After the event a few people said that our campaign was unnecessary, that the runway was such a silly idea that it would never have happened. That was not so. There was strong pressure from the airlines. Gatwick was clearly the front-runner in the RUCATSE report, and indeed BAA withdrew their support for the Heathrow option. If it had not been for our campaign, the Government might well have designated Gatwick as the preferred site even if construction was deferred.

Or the runway might have been built in an over-optimistic anticipation of future demand. That is what happened at Manchester. In 1997-2001 a second runway was built, despite a vigorous and sometimes violent environmental protest led by the troglodyte Swampy. It was designed to increase the capacity of the airport from 25 million passengers a year to 60 million but has proved a white elephant. Not just any old off-white elephant, a brilliant glossy-white elephant: the number of people using Manchester has fallen to below 20 million.

The need for a new runway in the South East is like the pot of gold at the end of the rainbow. The aviation industry is always desperate to get it. But when the real need is examined carefully it moves further and further away: in 1993 it was postponed to 2003; in the 2003 White Paper the new runway was to be built by 2012; in 2011 the forecasts showed there was no need for a new runway until 2030.

Julie Lowe recalls that our campaign was fun but immensely hard work: 'we had to do it because we all felt so threatened. *But I was angry, still am, at having to give up two years of my life.'*

Why is it that the captains of industry, who are paid enormous sums to do their jobs, are showered with peerages and knighthoods, while the unpaid volunteers who struggle to preserve our precious countryside and our heritage of ancient buildings for the benefit of future generations never get a gong?[66]

The Saxon insurgents
1066 – 1280

Mention of the wall paintings reminds me that I promised to explain my theory about why Charlwood church was built, so please forgive a light-hearted digression. When I give talks on the history of Charlwood church, many people ask me to write down my speculation. So for what it is worth, here it is.

At the time of the Norman Conquest, Charlwood lay in the middle of the Surrey-Sussex Weald, a wilderness of bogs and brambles. Apart from one circular field on the side of Norwood Hill, there is no evidence of a Saxon settlement. So why did the Normans, in around 1080, build a comparatively large church here?

It is often thought that when William had won the battle of Hastings he had conquered England. It was not so easy: there was still a great deal of Saxon resistance. William marched first to Canterbury and then, his scouts reporting that the bridges over the Thames in London were stoutly defended, marched west along the North Downs to Winchester. From there he moved to Wallingford, and crossed the Thames in order to take London from the north.[67]

After Hastings the Saxons mounted a half-hearted rear-guard action, at a site not yet discovered by archaeologists, following which the remnants of Harold's army must have dispersed into the Weald. Williams of Poitiers, writing c.1070 describes how they fled from the battle 'some on horses they had seized, some on foot; some along roads, others through untrodden wastes.'[68] Some may have slunk off home, others camped out in the woods. There they may have been joined by the stragglers from Harold's rapid march down from Yorkshire. Indeed it is recorded that at the battle of Hastings Harold had available only one third or one half of his intended force. The stragglers and survivors would have been horrified and enraged by the reports of the burning, looting, and rape carried out by the Normans. The Normans, according to one of the main historic sources, 'laid waste Sussex, Kent, Hampshire, Middlesex and Hertforshire, and did not cease from burning townships and slaying men.'[69]

Perhaps some remnants of the Saxon army eventually congregated in the woods and 'untrodden wastes' around Charlwood, and waged guerrilla war from there. The village at that time may have been a local centre for the smelting and forging of iron. (In one of the runway campaigns a friendly geologist pointed out a piece of iron slag in our church wall built in around 1280.) Charlwood would have been a good strategic position, cut off from most directions by the River Mole and by two tributary streams, Deanoak Brook and Mans Brook, cut deep into the soft clay which, as I know from my foxhunting days, would have been virtually impassable for knights and their horses. Perhaps the name 'Charlwood' - the wood of the men who owed allegiance to no lord - made it a natural place to rally, or perhaps the village acquired its name at that time.

In the five years after the Conquest, as is well documented, William had to undertake campaigns to subdue the Saxons in the West Country, in the north of England, in Herefordshire, and in Ely where Hereward the Wake took his last stand. The men of Kent 'goaded by Norman oppression'[70] plotted to seize Dover castle.

There is no written evidence, so far as I know, of a similar uprising in the Weald but it is my supposition that Charlwood became a centre for what would now be called 'insurgents', and that a contingent of Norman troops was also sent down to round them up. Afterwards, as happened elsewhere in England, the church would have been built by forced Saxon labour to impress and subdue the locals. Indeed the church, with its high slit window, thick walls and strong squat tower, could well have doubled as the defendable barracks for the local Norman militia.

This theory is slightly buttressed by two facts. First, that Charlwood parish became a 'peculiar', a detached outlying parish, of Canterbury. Second, that despite its comparatively large church, Charlwood is not mentioned in the Domesday Book, compiled in 1085. The Saxon church at Worth, about five miles south east of Charlwood, was recorded.

Maybe Charlwood church had not been built by Domesday time, but one would still expect to find a sizeable settlement worthy of inclusion in such a comprehensive survey. The explanation given in various books on local history is that Charlwood was a sub-manor of Merstham (about eight miles north of Charlwood). The Domesday Book shows that the Archbishop of Canterbury held Merstham 'for himself, for the clothing of the monks. Before 1066 Merstham answered for 20 hides; now for 5 hides.'[71] A hide was about 120 acres, and the reduction in the area of farmland was probably a sign of the ravages caused by the Norman Conquest – indeed Merstham lay on the route taken by William's army from Canterbury to Winchester.

Merstham was recorded as having one church and a population of 21 villagers, 4 smallholders and 8 slaves (slavery was common in Saxon times but died out soon after the Conquest). It hardly looks likely that this included Charlwood. Therefore my supposition is that perhaps Charlwood was excluded because it had acquired a reputation as a centre for Saxon resistance.

It is my further supposition that in the following centuries

Charlwood church became something of a place of unofficial pilgrimage to the memory of Saxon England. Footpaths lead to the church for ten miles across country from all directions. Charlwood remained rebellious, and refused to recognise the Archbishop of Canterbury, Thomas Becket, when he returned from exile in 1170. On Christmas Day the Archbishop excommunicated the Rector of Charlwood, along with a number of bishops. 'May they all be damned by Jesus Christ' he intoned as he took flaming candles from the altar and hurled them to the floor.[72]   Four days later the Archbishop was murdered in his cathedral.

Another piece of evidence for my theory lies in the church murals, painted around 1280-1300. Whereas many churches have paintings showing the day of judgment, the Charlwood paintings tell various lively stories. One has to ask why the rector at that time chose these particular subjects.

The main picture tells the story of St Margaret.   A heathen lord asks her to marry him, or more likely to share his bed that night. As a good Christian, she refuses. He throws her into prison. She is tempted by the devil in the form of a dragon. He says to her: 'Be a sensible girl; just lie on your back and shut your eyes.' When she rejects this friendly advice the devil-dragon swallows her. She makes a sign of the cross inside the creature's belly and miraculously pops out. It was a fashionable moral tale in the Middle Ages, and St Margaret became, somewhat illogically, the patron saint of women in childbirth.[73]

In the Charlwood painting, however, it is easy to see that the lord is a Norman knight, out hunting on his horse with his greyhound chasing a hare (the earliest picture of hare hunting in England), with his very Norman standard bearer out in front. St Margaret can be seen as a fair-haired Saxon lass resisting his advances, determined to keep her racial purity. (Even in recent times miscegenation was a crime in many American States, which is why Barack Obama was born in Hawaii). Margaret's prison sufferings could be seen as those of the Saxon populace, and her miraculous escape their hope.

The end of the wall-painting story is, however, curiously tragic. Margaret is tried in a court where the judge orders her to be executed, her head is cut off and her soul in the shape of a dove is seen flying up to heaven. While this final scene does occur in the standard version of the legend, the hidden message would not have been lost on the pro-Saxon congregation: that in Norman England there was no justice for the innocent. As twelfth-century writer Orderic Vitalis recorded: 'Meanwhile, the English were groaning under the Norman yoke ... the [Norman lords] were so swollen with pride that they would not deign to hear the reasonable plea of the English or give them impartial judgement. When their men at arms were guilty of plunder and rape they protected them by force, and wreaked their wrath all the more violently upon those who complained of the cruel wrongs they suffered.'[74]

Another Charlwood wall painting shows three princes meeting three skeletons. The skeletons utter a grim sound bite. 'As you are, we were. As we are, you will be.' The story of the Three Living and the Three Dead was popular in the Middle Ages, especially after the black death: fourteen other churches in England have a similar picture. But the Charlwood picture was painted before the black death, and Charlwood is the only church in which the princes are on horseback, one with a hawk on his wrist. They are clearly Norman knights and I like to suppose that the clandestine message to the Saxon congregation is that sure enough in due course the Normans will get their comeuppance.

Admittedly the walls were painted two hundred years after the Conquest, but folk memories live long, especially in relation to land seizure. One only has to think of Kosovo where the Serbs are still re-living the battle of 1389 against the Ottoman Turks, or Northern Ireland where resentment at the Protestant settlements has continued for hundreds of years and cost thousands of lives. The fact that people feel a semi-mystical link to the land of their fathers is a factor in runway battles, even if not one factored into the cost-benefit calculations of the Transport Department statisticians.

Indeed when one is considering the potential deso-lation of an historic village there is also the churchyard to consider. Around 10,000 people, including our Saxon forebears, are probably buried in Charlwood churchyard, and a number of their descendents still live in the village. The calculation is simple, and applies to any ancient country churchyard. Age of churchyard 930 years. Average life expectancy say 40 years (perhaps less taking account of the large number of infant deaths). Number of generations 23. Average population around 500. Deduct a few for cremations in the past century, and QED, as we used to write in our school mathematics homework, around 10,000 people are buried in the churchyard, most of them waiting in confident expectation of rising out of their graves on the Day of Judgement.

All my speculation about the Saxon origins of Charlwood church is based on circumstantial evidence with no forensic proof. It is a light-hearted digression: back to the serious business of dealing with an expanding airport.

CHARLWOOD PLACE · REV HY WISE ..   J. HASSELL 1823

Taming the airport
1994 – 2011

An airport is an exciting place. Those romantic destinations. The aircraft, sleek masterpieces of technology. The impressive safety record. The passengers, all ages, all races, all manners of mankind, measured in their millions. The aircrew in their stylish uniforms. At Gatwick over 20,000 people working on the airport, working for common purpose, a marvel of organisation.

Not surprising therefore that, as seen from the management offices on the seventh floor of the South Terminal, there may be a slight sense of disdain for the lesser mortals who live in the surrounding area, left behind in the march of progress.

There is no comprehensive legislation governing the environmental impact of aircraft or airports. In 1922 the infant aviation industry was given exemption from prosecution from noise, and airlines have always enjoyed a privileged legal status. Section 78 of the Civil Aviation Act 1982 gives the Secretary of State for Transport power to make regulations to limit the 'noise and vibration' from aircraft, but few regulations have been made. One of the few ways in which an airport can be tamed is that when a planning application is submitted, a public inquiry is held, and the independent Inspector may be persuaded to impose conditions.

During the late 1990's a number of public inquiries were held relating to Gatwick. One was into the Crawley Local Plan which defined how far the airport could expand towards Charlwood; another was into the diversion of the River Mole; and another was into BAA plans, now defunct, to build a visitor centre designed to become one of the biggest tourist attractions in the South East. The main attraction was to have been model aircraft simulators to enable punters to play at being a pilot and see if they could land at their destination airport without crashing - not good for the nerves of passengers waiting to board. At each inquiry I led the unofficial opposition, working closely with the planning officers, especially Jack Straw from Mole Valley and John Phillips from Tandridge, and enjoyed playing at being a barrister, cross-examining the rival witnesses.

Over the years we managed to obtain some important con-ditions: huge earth banks to protect Charlwood and Hookwood; a barrier to prevent our villages becoming a rat-run to a back entrance of the airport; a wavy wall to protect Horley from noise.

BAA started talking about expanding the airport by 50 per cent, from 27 million passengers to 40 million. The plans involved extending the terminals, providing new aircraft park-ing stands, building a new hangar and a new cargo area. Each would have involved a separate public inquiry but with little hope of success.

To seek a solution GACC organised a seminar in March 1998 at Gravetye Manor, an upmarket country hotel near East Grinstead whose owner hated the aircraft which destroyed the peace of his fine medieval house and garden – hated them so much that he gave us the use of the hotel and a haute cuisine meal for free. All the local MPs and top council people came – not least because they knew the food would be superb. We worked out the idea of a legal agreement whereby the councils would grant planning permis-sion for all the airport developments within the airport boundary in exchange for a comprehensive set of environmental protections.

My purpose was partly Machiavellian. If we could get a new legal agreement signed and generally welcomed, it would be harder for the Government to revoke the existing legal agreement, signed in 1979, that no new runway could be constructed before 2019.

The trouble curiously came with West Sussex County Council and Crawley Borough Council which were the planning authorities. Their planning officers had no wish to see their responsibility diminished, and went into an uncooperative sulk. Fortunately Neil Matthewson was by now one of the leading councillors on West Sussex. He read the riot act, and the project proceeded.

Janis Kong, Director of Gatwick, was keen on the idea. She had no wish to go through another inquiry like the Heathrow four year marathon.[75]   Thus I found myself having regular tête-à-têtes with Janis in her office looking down the Gatwick runway, and sitting on the sofa alongside her fluffy toys. With quiet but firm discussion we managed to resolve a number of the most difficult issues. The key concession by the airport was to promise that the area within the 57 leq contour – the area affected by serious noise – would be halved.

Eventually the agreement was signed in February 2001, and acclaimed by BAA as a major achievement. In their annual report they devoted a whole page to a mock apology to the legal profession. *'Something rather extraordinary has happened at Gatwick. Without resorting to the courts, BAA has reached a legally-binding agreement with the local authorities.... No confrontation. No public inquiries. No interminable delays, or arguments between opposing lawyers... We recognise that this new approach to planning may come as something of a blow to the legal profession, but we rather hope it may catch on.'*[76]

Janis went on to become director of Heathrow, a director of Network Rail, and, less happily, a non-executive director of the Royal Bank of Scotland before it went bust. She still records on her cv that she was 'previously managing director of Gatwick Airport, where she led the airport's groundbreaking partnership approach to community and stakeholder consultation.'

To assist the negotiations along, BAA confirmed that they accepted the 1979 no runway legal agreement. At the time that appeared to them and to us as merely a statement of the obvious: BAA had to abide by the law. It was therefore with a twinge of contrition that we found the Competition Commission some years later quoting this passive acceptance as a reason for breaking up BAA and forcing the sale of Gatwick.

The fact that we had been able to reach an environmentally friendly and legally binding agreement with BAA was because, although privatised, BAA plc retained some of the ethos that it was a public body with a duty to serve the public interest, which included being nice to local residents. That was soon to change.

In 2006 BAA was bought by a Spanish construction company, Ferrovial, which had started life, as its iron way name implies, by building railways. They were able to buy Gatwick on the cheap by exploiting a Spanish tax dodge that gave a 25 per cent subsidy on foreign take-overs.[77] The EU had ruled this subsidy illegal but it was not phased out until several years later.

At Gatwick the main effect was that most of the senior staff were sacked. We were particularly sorry to say good-bye to the airport director Paul Griffiths who, like Janis Kong, had proved a good friend and sympathetic to environmental issues. We had invited him to visit Charlwood church: he remained unmoved when we pointed out the Norman arches, the medieval wall-paintings and the Tudor screen but went into raptures when he discovered the historic Holdich organ. It emerged that he was a leading church organist, and – until the Ferrovial takeover – he was lined up to give an organ recital in Charlwood church. Since he left he has been running Dubai airport, with nearly twice as many passengers as Gatwick, the largest airport terminal in the world, and no green belt to worry about. Surprisingly he has managed to combine that job with being Chairman of the Royal College of Organists. Not everyone in the aviation industry is a wicked Philistine!

When the new (2001) agreement ran out in 2009 the West Sussex and Crawley planning officers thought they knew all the answers, and declined to involve GACC. Ferrovial pulled the wool well and truly over their eyes. In exchange for the councils undertaking in effect not to object to airport planning applications Ferrovial agreed to produce 'action plans' on noise, pollution and other matters. 'Action plans' sounded good and the planners took no notice when we pointed out that an action plan - with no description of what the action was to be - was not worth a row of legal beans.

As a result of a diktat by the Competition Commission, in December 2009 Ferrovial sold Gatwick to a faceless international consortium led by Global Infrastructure Partners. Again most of the senior staff were sacked, and a new American management style arrived with a relentless pursuit of profit.

BAA plc had been a British company, with mainly British shareholders, publishing a full annual report and holding an annual general meeting in London, attended by several thousand shareholders. That made them sensitive to pressure from environmental groups or local MPs. By contrast the owners of Gatwick are now hedge funds and pension funds based in New York, Abu Dhabi, Korea, California, and Australia.

They met their match, however, in Ann Jones, an elderly, white-haired lady from East Grinstead. She was annoyed by aircraft noise and had adopted the unusual, some would say eccentric, tactic of telephoning the airport noise complaints service each time an aircraft passed near her house.

In around 2005 BAA sent the police to caution her. She continued to press the redial button.

The kind organ-playing airport director went to see her. She continued to press the redial button.

Ferrovial sent the police (in what she described as 'riot gear') to arrest her, and she was fined. She continued to press the redial button.

When Global Infrastructure Partners took over, they had the police arrest her again, and she was charged with the criminal offence of causing annoyance by using a telephone.[78] Since she was only speaking to an answerphone in a department established with the purpose of receiving complaints, it did not seem the most heinous of crimes. She got in touch with GACC, and we managed to obtain excellent legal advice.[79] After many months delay, when anxiety caused her health to deteriorate, she appeared in court, a frail little lady in the dock surrounded with armour-plated glass.

She was accused of trying to annoy the airport but replied that she was not annoying the airport: it was their aircraft that were annoying her. Each of her calls was shown to refer to a specific aircraft. She was accused of using bad language, but there was nothing that would have shocked Jane Austen. She was accused of the crime of using up space on the answerphone tape but replied that it would be nicer if she could sometimes speak to a real person. The magistrates threw the case out, declaring her not guilty and, by implication, Global Infrastructure Partners guilty of heavy-handed bullying and wasting police time. She is still pressing the redial button.

But that is to jump ahead in time. We need to back-space ten years to the runway issue, and to yet another serious threat to destroy the village of Charlwood.

THE CAGE

We Trust in the Law
1999 – 2002

It will be recalled that the outcome of RUCATSE was to postpone a decision. The search for new runways was taken up in March 1999. The Minister of Transport, John Reid, announced a new series of regional airport studies of which the main one was the South East Regional Airport Study - SERAS. This time GACC was not invited onto the official committee – perhaps we had asked too many awkward questions last time round.

Our situation was much weaker. A Labour Government had been elected. We had no friends in the Cabinet. All the local MPs, bar one, were Tories, and it would have given the Government no qualms to put a new runway in their constituencies. The one Labour MP was Laura Moffat, the Member for Crawley, whose husband worked at the airport: not surprisingly, she was in favour of airport expansion.

We were consulted on the SERAS draft terms of reference, and replied they contained no mention of legal commitments. It soon became clear that the civil servants in the Transport Department believed that their job was solely to identify the best places, from the point of view of aviation and geography, to put new runways. They took the view that the legal agreement prohibiting any new runway at Gatwick was a minor political issue to be dealt with later by the politicians. The 'unequivocal assurance' that there would never be a second runway at Stansted was another foolish pledge made by politicians and not worthy of consideration by high-minded public servants.

One point that stood out a mile was that it was foolish to base the need for airport expansion for the next thirty years on forecasts of future demand with no reference to the future price of air travel: the first lesson learnt by any student of economics is that demand depends on the price. It was time to put my rusty economics to use.

I therefore wrote a small booklet *Airports Policy – A Flawed Approach* which was published by the Aviation Environment Federation in April 2000 with support from Friends of the Earth and from our friends at Stansted. It pointed out that air travel was remarkably cheap, mainly due to tax advantages compared to other industries and the absence of taxes related to environmental damage.   In doing my research for this book, and looking up the Cabinet papers relating to Maplin, I have found that I was not the first to make the point. In 1971 the Home Secretary (and former Chancellor) Reggie Maudling reported to Ted Heath and his Cabinet the Treasury belief that 'there is strong fiscal discrimination in favour of air travel, which is substantially free of tax .... In view of the environmental problems created by the growth of the industry, this seems unjustifiable to the Treasury who believe that a study should be put in hand of the possibilities and probable consequences of seeking to slow down the growth of air traffic by fiscal means.'[80]

No such study was ever put in hand, and My *Flawed Approach* booklet, followed by another called *Tax-free Aviation*, made no dent in the Transport Department's determination to support aviation growth.

The inexorable pressure from the airlines and from government led to a consolidation of the green opposition. In 2000 our loose federation of national environmental groups plus airport protest groups was given a name – the somewhat uninspiring title of 'AirportWatch'. It brought together CPRE –The Campaign for the Protection of Rural England (I had become chairman of their aviation policy group), Transport 2000 (now the Campaign for Better Transport), Friends of the Earth, Greenpeace, RSPB, the Woodland Trust, the World Wildlife Fund (now WWF-UK), the Aviation Environment Federation and airport protest groups from around the UK.[81] The National Trust and the World Development Movement gave semi-detached moral support. The dynamic chairman was John Stewart, veteran of the road protests at Twyford Down and Newbury, and chairman of HACAN, the Heathrow environmental group. I threw in my experience of politics and government.

The Transport Department remained adamant and impervious. The whole SERAS study was undertaken by consultants who used their computer mapping systems to locate every two mile stretch of flat land in the South East suitable for a runway. Not just land– they also looked at the idea of an island in the Thames Estuary, rejecting it in half a dozen sentences as too far from London.

One morning a man was seen taking photos of houses in Charlwood. Under cross-examination (we have our methods), he admitted he was employed by one of the consultancy firms and was surveying the line of a new runway. Scary.

Representatives from environmental groups met the civil servants to discuss the preliminary SERAS findings, but made little impression on them. After the meeting we repaired to the café next door, and who should come in but the Secretary of State, John Reid – explaining that he had to get out of his office for a quick smoke. So we had a useful chat. A lobbying company would have charged thousands for that opportunity.

It was not possible for GACC to launch a campaign while these secret studies were in progress. You cannot ask the public to oppose an investigation. It was obvious to us, however, that a new runway at Gatwick was likely to feature large in the eventual proposals; and that the legal agreement was going to be crucial.

Neil Matthewson skilfully persuaded the West Sussex county councillors to pass a resolution pledging to uphold the agreement, thus blocking off the scope for the Government to induce or bribe them (knighthoods are a cheap form of bribery) to bring forward the end date of the legal agreement from 2019.

Because we had plenty of time to prepare, we were able to persuade over a hundred councils and local environmental and amenity groups to sign a statement of support for the legal agreement – and each to send us a photo of their town or village. These were put together in an attractive booklet: *We Trust in the Law*. As well as listing all the bodies which supported the agreement, the booklet spelt out in words of one syllable the difficulty which a government would face if it wished to overturn the agreement – the need for a hybrid Bill with protracted debates in the Commons, and the likelihood that the House of Lords (as with Stansted in 1965) would throw the Bill out. The booklet was to have a decisive influence.

Somehow we arranged for copies of the booklet to be given out to all those attending the first meeting of the SERAS steering group. Our main concern, however, was to get the booklet to the ministers who would be making the crucial decisions. As I knew from having spent four years sitting next door to a Cabinet Minister's private office, civil servants are well trained not to bother their bosses with what they regard as petty propaganda. If we posted the booklet to the Minister, his private secretary would send us a polite acknowledgement while dropping the booklet disdainfully in the rubbish bin.

It happened, however, that there was a Parliamentary debate on some aviation issue. The debate took place in a House of Commons Committee Room, and when it concluded, the Minister came over to chat to the public. I seized the opportunity and handed him *We Trust in the Law*, saying: '*This is what your civil servants won't let you see.*' He tucked it under his jacket, replying: '*I won't show it to them!*'

A huge amount of analysis was done by the consultants and we waited agog. The results were published in a consultation document in July 2002.[82]   UK demand for air travel was forecast to expand from 181 million passengers a year in 2000 to 501 million in 2030. Plans were produced for an extra runway at Heathrow, and for either one extra runway at Stansted, or two extra runways at Stansted, or (unbelievably) three extra runways at Stansted. And plans were set out in colourful detail for an entirely new airport with five (yes five!) runways at Cliffe, on the Thames marshes in Kent – the site that the Gatwick Protest Committee had suggested to Harold Macmillan back in 1954.

Agog turned to astonishment when we discovered that Gatwick hardly featured at all. The chapter on Gatwick was relegated to Appendix F. The main document merely stated that the legal agreement prevented start of construction of any new runway before 2019, and that: 'The Government does not intend to overturn that agreement' and in bold **'Government will not, therefore, include in the White Paper any options for new runways at Gatwick.'**

We could hardly believe our luck. Later we heard from a senior civil servant that it was the Prime Minister, Tony Blair, who had taken the decision to exclude Gatwick. The chapter on Gatwick in Appendix F looked a cut and paste job, indicating that the decision had been taken at a very late stage, probably at the final Cabinet meeting. We won't know for sure until the Cabinet Minutes for 2002 are published in 2032.

Strict orders were issued to GACC supporters that any champagne was to be drunk in private so as not to anger our friends at Heathrow and Stansted who faced such horrific proposals. The celebration did not last long. Crawley Borough councillors, pompously proud of their civic dignity, were upset that Gatwick was consigned to an appendix. Not even Appendix A. F was the final insult to their pride. A powerful group of lawyers from Stansted applied for judicial review of the Gatwick decision. They were supported by Kent County Council who disliked the Cliffe proposal, and – to our astonishment – by Crawley Council.

For three days I sat in the High Court, next to my old friend and opposite number from Stansted, Norman Meade. As a founder member of our long-standing non-aggression treaty, he was somewhat abashed. He briefed his barristers while I found myself in the curious position of briefing the Government barristers defending the exclusion of Gatwick. To my surprise, much turned on *We Trust in the Law*. The top civil servant dealing with airports policy gave evidence that the Government had relied on it. Crawley Borough Council told the court that they had never agreed to have their name included in our booklet. I rushed home and managed to find evidence that, although they had not agreed to sign the booklet, they had supported the legal agreement. The outcome, however, was that the judge ruled that Gatwick should have been included in the consultation, and the Government were forced to rewrite the consultation document.

The rewriting process, and putting the Gatwick proposals through the Cabinet, took several months. While the Heathrow and Stansted protest groups launched their campaigns we were put into a state of suspended animation, unable to start our campaign until we knew exactly what we were to be threatened with.

A year or two earlier, as part of the earlier SERAS study, the Transport Department statisticians had invented a wonderful new computer model which proved conclusively what a huge demand there was going to be by 2030 for new runways, how many people would use a new runway at each proposed site, and the economic benefits of each. Since the results came out of a computer, ministers were unable to argue with them.

The statisticians, showing an unexpected sense of humour, named the computer model 'SPASM'. What the initials stood for is irrelevant: it was a beautiful baby and they were immensely proud of it. They invited everyone to come and admire it. After we had all leaned over the pram and said 'ooh' and 'ah' and 'isn't it lovely', I asked quietly from the back row: *'Would you be willing to run the SPASM model through again with a different set of assumptions?'* 'Yes, of course', they puffed with pride, *'the computer model is a very sophisticated device which can deal with different inputs. We can certainly do it for you after the consultation is published.'*

The interregnum, while we waited for the Gatwick runway plans, gave time for the Aviation Environment Federation (AEF) to pursue the SPASM offer. We carefully worked out a set of parameters to be fed into the computer: they could be summarised as an assumption that by 2030 air travel would be subject to the same rate of tax as car travel. 'Easy,' said the statisticians, 'we'll just feed them into the computer and after a few minutes the results will come out at the other end.' Six weeks went by and no results appeared. We threatened politely that we might need to mention the matter to the press. In due course we were given an unintelligible spreadsheet: when we had deciphered it the result was all we had hoped. SPASM proved that if air travel were to pay the same rate of tax as car travel, demand would be substantially reduced and no new runways would be required.

Meanwhile I had been writing another AEF booklet, this one titled The *Hidden Cost of Flying*. The benefit to the aviation industry of no tax on aircraft fuel and no VAT on anything to do with air travel, only slightly offset by air passenger duty, was calculated at £9 billion a year. Constant repetition of that figure over the following years (until it was overshadowed by the colossal sums needed to bail out the banks) put the aviation industry on the defensive.

Into the booklet, as it went to press, we spatchcocked a section on the SPASM rerun. The results made the front page of The Times and had the beneficial result of uniting the environmental movement. In their responses to the SERAS consultation the main national environmental organisations - The National Trust, The Woodland Trust, CPRE, Friends of the Earth, Greenpeace and Transport 2000 - all reiterated that with fair tax no new runways would be needed. The Government, egged on by a powerful aviation lobby group, took not the blindest notice.

No Way Gatwick Runway
2003

In February 2003 the revised consultation document was published including, to comply with the court order, various runway options for Gatwick. The options were: a close parallel runway; a so-called wide-spaced runway to the south of the airport; or two new runways, one to the south plus one to the north.

The southern runway was shown squeezed between the airport and Crawley. The plans showing the northern runway were similar to those in the 1993 RUCATSE report. Charlwood would have been left isolated, desolate and derelict between the new runway and the present runway. A cutting one kilometre wide and 50 metres deep would have been necessary through Stan Hill.

The two new runway option was designed to give Gatwick a capacity of 120 million passengers a year, twice the then size of Heathrow and four times the then size of Gatwick. In terms of noise, traffic, housing and industrial development it would have had a huge impact on the whole surrounding area, and would have altered the character of much of southern England.

This time our campaign slogan was 'No Way Gatwick Runway'. It was a funny sort of campaign because we knew that we were really supporting the Government in their original decision. It was difficult to persuade large numbers of the public to object or to turn out for demonstrations because most people felt that the Government had already taken the decision to rule Gatwick out. Yet we had to jump up and down a lot because the protest groups at Heathrow and Stansted were running massive public campaigns, and if we did not make a similar fuss some Cabinet members might conclude that people at Gatwick did not care as much.

In order to explain the new runway proposals, the Department for Transport put on an exhibition at the Hilton Hotel at Gatwick. We managed to book the next-door room and put on a rival exhibition. Each of the towns and villages most affected set up a stall. Because the civil servants were really on our side but couldn't say so, it was all very good humoured; the civil servants visited our exhibition and we visited theirs. We had lots of balloons with the slogan 'No Way Gatwick Runway'; when a small child started to cry in the Department's exhibition, a senior civil servant came into our room to ask for a balloon to cheer her up.

Neil Matthewson addressed umpteen town and village meetings. Peter Barclay gave umpteen television interviews outside the historic Half Moon pub in Charlwood. The vivacious Kathy Lewis organised the 'Charlwood Home Guard' to repel invasion, and the Home Guard put up huge notice boards to show the wide extent of the new runways. Our geese appeared in The Times to illustrate the rural peace that was about to be destroyed.

In Crawley a number of Labour councillors, appalled by the foolishness of their colleagues in helping to propel Gatwick into the firing line, joined forces with the Tories and Lib Dems to create a group called 'One's Enough' (meaning one runway). We had a series of jolly meetings with much wine, and by the end of the consultation period they succeeded in turning the Crawley council round and achieving a unanimous vote against any new runway.

Colin Gates, whose ancestors had lived in Charlwood since the 13th century, composed a bawdy runway song, which was belted out by the local lasses on all possible occasions, preferably in front of the TV cameras. The last line of the chorus, 'They don't care a bugger for the likes of you and me,' was judged by the BBC as fit for their news bulletins but the lasses got the giggles when ITV insisted on a bowdlerised version.

As a rule GACC does not go in for demonstrations, petitions or direct action. A handful of protesters holding placards outside an airport which handles 30 million passengers a year merely demonstrates weakness. Similarly a petition with a few thousand signatures looks insignificant compared to the half a million signatures obtained by the Countryside Alliance or the 1.5 million signatures on the Downing Street website against road pricing. Direct action by a small group of protesters, such as blocking an airport approach road, which results in annoying thousands of air passengers is equally likely to prove counterproductive. But by this stage in our campaign we felt a need to get something on television if only to hearten our own supporters – and to get press or TV coverage it is necessary to do something illegal or at least colourful.

To draw attention to the nonsense of putting a runway in a deep cutting Nick Hague organised a demonstration in Edolphs Copse, the bluebell wood which was due to disappear down the runway cutting. The Woodland Trust enthusiastically supported the demo. In order to get some dramatic pictures on the television news, five hundred people were assembled in front of a giant bulldozer and harangued by the local MP, Sir Paul Beresford. Those were the days before satellite news reporting: at the last minute the television channels told us they could not cover the story due to the difficulty on a Saturday afternoon of getting a motorcycle dispatch rider to deliver film from the site to the studio. Sadly our demo went largely unreported.

The main message, however, that the cutting through the hill would mean moving 25 times as much earth as the notorious cutting at Twyford Down was not lost on the politicians.   The Twyford Down and Newbury bypass demos had led to a rethink of the policy of unlimited road building. Our message was that a similar rethink was needed for airports policy.

West Sussex County Council, led by the commanding Lt. Col. Tex Pemberton, cabinet member for the Environment, campaigned alongside us. Tex and I found our paths had converged in the past: he had been in charge of Prime Minister Heath's military body guard at 10 Downing Street at the same time that I was trotting in and out of Number 11. By a curious coincidence Colin Gates had been one of the policemen on duty outside the famous door at the same time.

All the councils, whether boroughs, districts or parishes, took their responsibility seriously and held intense debates on the runway issue. In the end over 80 councils and local environmental or amenity groups voted to oppose the runway plans. None, apart from one parish council which had a dominant pilot as a member, supported the new runway.

Gravetye Manor again played a crucial role. We held meetings there roughly every six months attended by the local MPs and senior representatives from the county and district councils. It was an excellent venue because it brought together the county councils on neutral ground, and the food remained superb. Francis Maude, the Member for Horsham, took over the chairmanship of the meetings, demonstrating subtle political acumen. At these private and informal meetings we were able to plan our strategy for opposing the runway – so long as we finished in time for lunch.

GACC recognised that outside experts carried more weight than the views of protesters. We arranged for an eminent QC to write a Counsel's Opinion confirming that the legal agreement was watertight. A group of retired pilots wrote a report for us to show that a close parallel runway wouldn't work because of wake vortices. If a large plane took off on one runway the turbulence in the air behind it would have prevented a second aircraft from taking off or landing on the close runway for a certain time – so there would be no increase in the number of aircraft able to use the airport. That view was subsequently confirmed by the CAA and killed off the close parallel idea. The pilots also pointed out that the northern option with the runway in a cutting would pose risks to safety.

Meanwhile the plan for a huge new airport at Cliffe was strongly opposed by the RSPB. With 4 million members they carried political clout. But the clinching blow came when an aeronautical institution published a report warning of the danger of bird strikes. The aviation industry and their supporters in the Department for Transport didn't care a damn if the birds had their nesting habits disturbed but they reacted with alarm to any risk of them getting into the engines. That was the end of Cliffe.

The lesson we learnt from the birds at Cliffe was that it was not sufficient to talk about the damage to Norman churches or medieval houses: it was necessary to prove to the aviation industry that Gatwick would be an inefficient site. So we rushed out a booklet *Gatwick – why a new runway won't work*. It gave the technical arguments against each option: the close parallel would suffer from wake vortices; the so-called wide-spaced runway was actually very narrow-spaced with little room between the runways; and the northern runway could only operate one way, and would mean aircraft flying through a cutting with safety risks posed by turbulence. It was sent to the top people in all the main UK airlines.

We may never know if it had any impact but we achieved our aim of demonstrating vigorous opposition at Gatwick. When the decision came in December 2003, in the shape of the Air Transport White Paper, the Government confirmed their original view that two new runways were needed in South East England before 2019, and that the legal agreement ruled out a Gatwick runway in that time scale. A new runway at Stansted was proposed, to be followed by a new runway at Heathrow, with the possibility of a new Gatwick runway, to the south of the existing runway, to be held in reserve.

The specific reprieve for Charlwood came in two somewhat oblique sentences: *There would need to be very extensive and intrusive earthworks to accommodate the northern runway. There was very little support for this option, and the Government too does not support it.*[84]

Exactly fifty years after the 1953 fog deceit, the chickens had come home to roost. It was the distrust caused by that deceit which had led West Sussex County Council to insist on the legal agreement, and in the end that proved the decisive factor.

It would be wrong, however, to suggest that Gatwick was merely ruled out by a legal document signed in 1979. If Gatwick had been the front-runner, the Government could have introduced legislation to revoke the legal agreement. But in the voluminous studies carried out by the Transport Department consultants, Gatwick did not score highly. It did not offer scope to provide a new hub. And it scored worse than Stansted on the number of people who would be affected by noise.

The defenders of Charlwood and all the nearby towns and villages were again able to open the champagne – but quietly. When a TV camera man tried to take a photo of locals celebrating in the Rising Sun we had firmly to stand in front of his camera. It would not do to let our friends at Heathrow and Stansted think their misery was our joy.

In truth, GACC was not quite as optimistic as we made out. We realised that the white paper had kept open the option for a second Gatwick runway to be constructed if the Heathrow runway could not meet the environmental conditions. It looked touch-and-go whether Heathrow would meet the conditions which the Government had set relating to noise and pollution. Gatwick airport added to our worries by publishing in 2006 a master plan that showed a map of a new runway and a timetable leading up to construction to start in August 2019 – the month that the legal agreement expired.

Nevertheless we took the decision to claim that the Gatwick battle was won, the runway defeated. First, because this helped to end the blight and enabled people to get on with their lives in peace. Second, because one cannot keep one's troops at a permanent state of apprehension without them becoming bored. Like soldiers in a medieval army, they need to go home to help with the harvest. Third, because if one goes on talking about the possibility of a new runway too long the public come to accept it as inevitable. The more the press discuss it, the more the politicians take it seriously. Better to wait until the threat re-appears and then shout 'Shock! Horror!' and launch a new campaign. So we deliberately adopted a low profile.

We felt huge sympathy for the people around Stansted and around Heathrow: there but for the grace of God (and for the grace of a legal document signed in 1979) would we have been. And we were enormously grateful to them that (apart from that one judicial review lapse) throughout their hard fought battles from 2003 to 2010 they played by the non-aggression pact rules. Despite what must sometimes have been huge temptation, never once did they suggest that a new runway at Gatwick might be preferable. Thank you, all at Stansted. Thank you, all at Heathrow.

Putting the runway on the reserve list had the effect of lifting much of the blight that had hung over all the surrounding towns and villages since 1990. One result was that house prices in Charlwood nearly doubled. We thought of suggesting that those who had worked so hard to defeat the runway might be rewarded with a small part of the increase in house values – a modest 10% would have sufficed to make us all comfortable! Unfortunately the idea never took off.

The end of the blight also meant that we could resume plans to extend the church. The Normans and the Tudors had failed to provide a loo. In bygone days when everyone walked to church and could use the bushes in the churchyard that was not too serious. But, as in many other rural English parishes, what with women priests and with people driving long distances to baptisms, weddings and funerals, a loo had become essential. While we were at it, we also decided to build a small church room and kitchen. The project had started in 1999, but had had to be put on hold when it seemed possible that Charlwood church might finish up like the church at Lowfield Heath, standing forlorn alongside a runway amidst the ruins of a derelict village.

Following the White Paper we were able to finalise the plans, consult all the experts, and obtain planning permission and a faculty – not an easy process for a Grade 1 listed building that had not been altered since 1480. The Charlwood community, no longer having to parade in front of bulldozers, no longer having to write letters of objection, no longer having to provide a rent-a-crowd for the TV cameras, turned with joy to organising fund-raising events. Patrick Cox, as church treasurer, managed to raise over £400,000, and rightly insisted that the extension must be built in stone. I was given the pleasant task of acting as clerk of works, coping with architects and stone masons, archaeologists and skeletons. Much more fun than opposing runways! The new extension was opened by the Lord Lieutenant, Sarah (now Dame Sarah) Goad in June 2009.

Providence Chapel has proved more difficult. This unique wooden building that, as Nicholas Pevsner remarked, would not look out of place in the remotest part of East Kentucky, was originally constructed in Horsham as a barracks to house troops assembled to repel an invasion by Napoleon. With the end of the war in 1815, it was bought by a Charlwood farmer, re-erected next to his house and dedicated as a nonconformist chapel. It remains, at the end of a muddy lane, attractive but with a diminishing congregation. In recent years the farmer's house (listed grade 2, Charlwood does things in style) became a brothel. To prevent the chapel elders casting prurient eyes on the sinners entering the premises, the brothel owner planted a large leylandii hedge which threatened to damage the chapel woodwork. When he departed to reside elsewhere at Her Majesty's pleasure, the leylandii were razed with joy.

Restoration of the building, at an estimated cost of around

Portrait of Charwood

A booklet illustrating the historic houses and the lively community of Charlwood, with a foreword by the Queen's solicitor, played an important part in the 1993-4 campaign.

WE TRUST IN THE LAW

All seven local MPs and over a hundred councils and environmental groups expressed their determination that the legal agreement banning a second runway should be honoured.

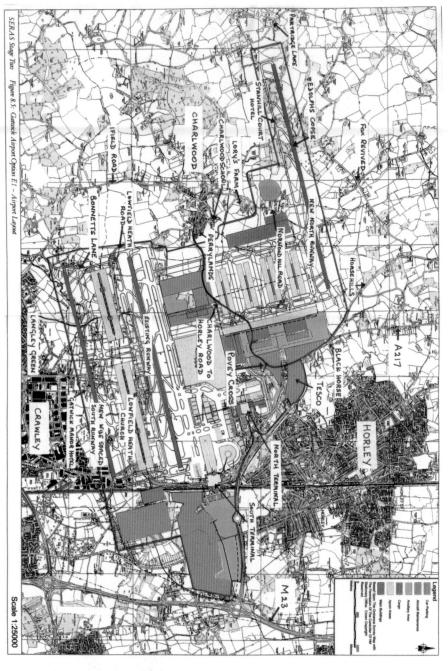

SERAS Stage Two   Figure 8.5: Gatwick Airport Option E1 – Airport Layout

Scale 1:25000

Following the court's decision that the Government must include Gatwick in the consultation, in 2003 a horrific plan was produced for Gatwick with three runways. If it had ever been implemented it would have destroyed Charlwood and totally altered the character of much of Surrey, Sussex and Kent.

The Government's decision to rule out Gatwick was challenged in the High Court (above). The court was told that the Government had relied on our 'Trust in the Law' booklet.

Gravetye Manor played a central role in co-ordinating anti-runway campaigns by MPs and local councils.

To show the nonsense of building a runway through a cutting in a hill, 500 people assembled to face a bulldozer in Edolphs Copse.

To produce a picture suitable for TV showing the extent of opposition we organised a photoshoot in Rusper. Local mothers and their children were recruited to hold the placards.

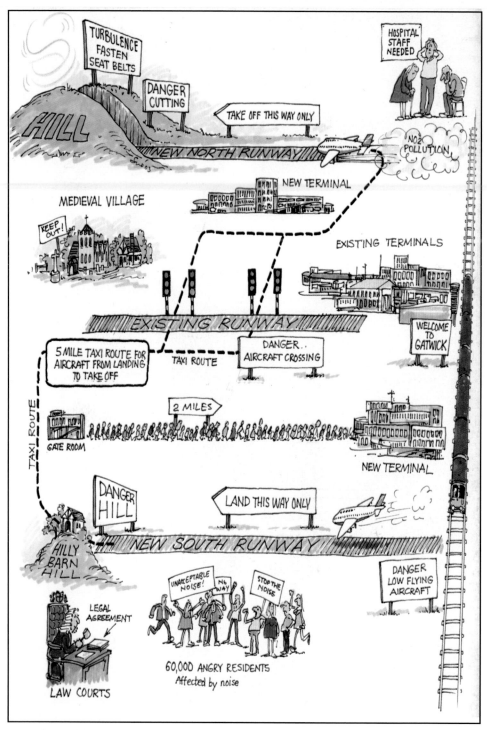

We emphasised the practical reasons why the Gatwick runway plans wouldn't work. The constrictions of the site meant that the airport would be exceptionally inefficient.

Gatwick –
destroying climate change targets

A study of the emissions caused by aircraft using Gatwick Airport

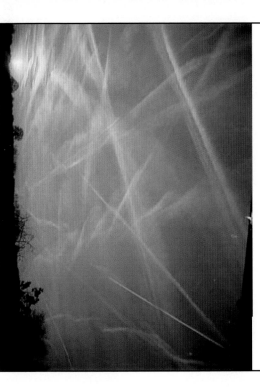

Contrails over Gatwick

Climate change was becoming a more serious issue. In this booklet we were able to show that aircraft using Gatwick caused more climate change damage than the total of all other human activities in the whole of Surrey and West Sussex.

Wreck the sky when you fly

On average each passenger on a return flight from Gatwick is responsible for the emission of sufficient CO2 gas to fill 47,000 party balloons.

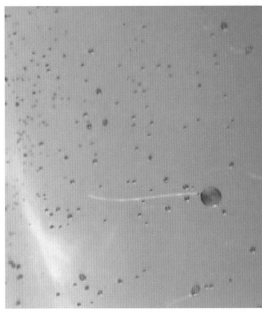

For every minute that each passenger is airborne they cause the emission of sufficient CO2 gas to fill about 195 party balloons.

Aircraft emissions (or balloons) are at least twice as damaging as the same amount at ground level.

CO2 remains is the atmosphere for up to 100 years, so each year more and more accumulates.

Our attempts to make air passengers feel guilty about the damage they were causing fell on deaf ears.

Neil Matthewson, chairman of GACC 1980-90, led the opposition to the North Terminal and, as a cabinet member of West Sussex County Council, persuaded the Council to uphold the no runway legal agreement.

Julie Lowe, chairman of the Charlwood Society, played a leading role in organising opposition to the 1993 runway plans.

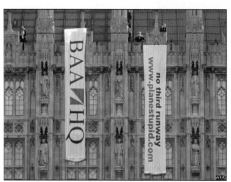

Young people, alarmed at the climate change damage caused by aviation, and at the aviation industry's undue influence on government, resorted to dramatic protests, such as hanging these banners on the Houses of Parliament.

When the runway blight was lifted, we were able to concentrate on building a new loo and meeting room for the church - the first extension since 1480.

John Byng who represents GACC on the airport consultative committee.

For the past ten years Peter Barclay has been the public face of GACC, appearing regularly on TV.

GATWICK – why a new runway won't work

A close parallel runway was ruled out because of wake vortices.

Fallible Forecasts
A critique of the 2007 air passenger forecasts

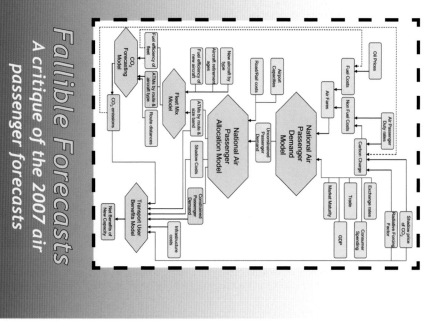

Official forecasts of the need for new runways were based on unrealistic assumptions, for example, that the price of oil would remain at 22p a litre until 2080.

Francis Maude, MP for Horsham, assured us that a pledge of no new runway at Gatwick would be included in the 2010 Tory manifesto. The Lib Dems had already made that promise.

When David Cameron and Nick Clegg formed a coalition Government the agreed policy included no second runway at Gatwick.

Celebrating the renovation of Bristow's Cottage - the Charlwood village school from 1620 to 1852. The cottage now belongs to a local charity and the rent goes towards education for Charlwood children. But what does the future hold for them and for their village?

£200,000, has become urgent.   English Heritage has expressed concern about the future of this building which is listed grade 2*, a listing which puts it among the top 6 per cent of historic buildings in Britain. The Heritage Lottery Fund offered to provide most of the money but the nonconformist chapel trustees turned this down because they believed that it would be sinful to accept money derived from gambling. Conservation can be uphill work!

The chapel was put on the market in August 2012 but, thanks to some nimble footwork to discourage potential purchasers, no offers were received. A new trust, with members drawn from the Charlwood History Group and with myself as chairman, has been set up to take on the ownership of the chapel and to organise its restoration.

PROVIDENCE CHAPEL

Fly Now, Grieve Later
2003 – 2010

The 2003 Air Transport White Paper represented a severe setback for the national environmental organisations. They had been defeated by a powerful campaign run by the airline lobbying group, 'Freedom to Fly', set up by British Airways, Virgin, BAA, the CBI and a number of trade unions.

The airlines had long experience of lobbying governments around the world. From the 1920's onwards they had managed to maintain exemption from any prosecution for noise. They had successfully maintained a virtually tax-free status in all countries. They had managed to stay out of international agreements to limit climate change damage. They started with the advantage of being able to offer journalists and MPs free flights to far-off places. And they had natural allies in the travel correspondents of the press: anyone reading the travel supplements was bound to get the message that to fly was to enjoy unlimited sun and sex.

The Transport Department saw its mission as being to improve transport, and that obviously meant building more roads and bigger airports. The Department has also always had a direct responsibility for maintaining the prosperity of the aviation industry, so the airport and airline executives were their natural allies.

Conversely the environmental groups started with several disadvantages. The civil servants were reluctant to have meetings with environmentalists who always seemed cast in the role of being opponents of government policy. The cartoon image of sandals and beards did not help. Nor did the tendency to resort to direct action. Breaking the law in order to draw attention to a pending environmental disaster is an excellent method of getting good press coverage, but is a switch-off for civil servants who cannot be found to be talking to criminals, anarchists or trouble-makers.

After the publication of the 2003 Air Transport White Paper a conference of dejected national environmental organisations was held to decide what to do next. The general view was that experience confirmed that it was no good merely defending our home ground; it was not sufficient to expound the value of protecting the countryside, preserving peace and quiet, or looking after wildlife; not sufficient even to draw attention to the growing climate change damage done by aviation: these tended to be over-ruled by the economic arguments – the need to provide jobs, the need to build new runways to cope with the apparently inexorable growth in air travel, and the calculations which showed that the economic value of new runways exceeded their environmental cost. If we were to win, it was necessary to defeat the economic arguments.

An Aviation Economics Committee was formed, with myself as chairman plus experts from the various national environmental organisations. Our first target was a report by Oxford Economic Forecasting Ltd (OEF).[86] The use of the word Oxford was clever, implying that it was part of the university and therefore academically respectable. Which it wasn't. The OEF report had been commissioned jointly by the airlines and the Department for Transport, but the airlines had paid 90 per cent of the cost. The consultants knew who was paying the piper and had produced a report that read like a publicity blurb for the industry. But it had been swallowed uncritically by the civil servants and regurgitated verbatim in the White Paper. We were able to show that it contained serious errors – all exaggerating the case for airport expansion.

For a time it looked as if international concern about climate change would put a stop to the growth in air travel. A number of reports from the United Nations panel of scientific experts (IPPC) between 1990 and 2001 had drawn attention to the fact that the increasing concentration of CO_2 in the atmosphere would have disastrous consequences for mankind.[87] A further IPPC report firmly nailed aviation as one of the chief culprits.[88] Aircraft engines emitted a large amount of CO_2. Scientists suggested (but are now less certain) that emissions in the upper atmosphere did somewhere between 2 and 4 times more damage than at ground level. Unlike coal-fired power stations, there was no technology in sight to solve the problem. And air travel was increasing ever upward.

The Tyndall Centre, a partnership of scientists from eight UK universities, came up with the calculation that, at the then rate of growth, by 2100 aircraft emissions would use up over 100 per cent of the UK's safe allowance of CO_2. In a booklet *'Fly now, grieve later'* I tried to set out the issues in non-technical language. A more academically respectable contribution to the debate was a detailed study on aviation entitled *'Predict and Decide'* by Dr Sally Cairns and Carey Newson of (the real) Oxford University. Polls began to show that the public were beginning to worry that flying was anti-social. The Bishop of London preached that to fly was to sin.

Down at Gatwick we dreamt up a stunt. We sought permission from BAA to take photographs of a mock passenger checking-in with 85 one-kilo bags of sugar – which we had calculated as equivalent in weight to the carbon released per passenger on an average air journey from Gatwick. BAA refused permission. Caroline Lucas, then a Green MEP (now an MP) and a good friend of GACC, repeated the request and offered to come along. Again BAA refused. We discussed whether to proceed without giving notice, but realised that the trolley load of sugar bags would immediately be suspected of being a bomb designed to blow up the airport terminal and that we would probably be shot by armed guards. There was a marked shortage of volunteers.

There was also a marked reluctance by the public to reduce their addiction to flying. To save the planet by recycling waste or installing solar panels or insulating the loft were all OK but foregoing a holiday on the sunny Mediterranean was to ask too much. A constant drip of semi-dishonest publicity by the airlines, combined with the fanatic evangelism of the climate change sceptics, backed up by the Daily Telegraph which depended on the airlines for its advertising revenue, enabled most members of the public to put their environmental consciences on hold while passing through the Gatwick departure lounge.

The campaigns against new runways at Heathrow and Stansted were gathering strength. At Gatwick we were still working hard to keep up a low profile, but were increasingly worried that the press and politicians might at any moment switch their attention to us. We could not defeat the underlying threat of new runways unless we also defeated the basic case for expansion - that the official forecasts produced by the Department for Transport statisticians showed air travel as due to more than double by 2030.

When I was studying economic statistics sixty years ago I did not understand much of the algebra but one thing I did learn was that with any mechanical model if you put rubbish in, you get rubbish out. And it seemed to me that the Transport statisticians were putting a good deal of rubbish into their forecasting model. For starters, they assumed that the cost of oil was going to fall from 27p a litre, as it was in 2007, to 22p in 2012 and stay at around that level until 2030. And until 2050. And until 2080.

The second big rubbish assumption was that there would be no change to the taxation of air travel. The Transport statisticians blithely fed into their computer that there would continue to be nil tax on aviation fuel until 2080. And no VAT. And that air passenger duty would continue at its comparatively low level. (Despite the unprincipled campaigns run by the airlines and the right wing press, air passenger duty only raises £3 billion a year compared to the £12 billion lost as a result of the absence of fuel tax and VAT.) Any motorist comparing that assumption to the tax on petrol could see that it was high-octane nonsense. There were several other unrealistic assumptions. We spelt them out in another booklet *Fallible Forecasts* published by GACC as a contribution to the general campaign.[90]

It all had no noticeable impact on government ministers: for fear of losing face they could not admit that their Air Transport White Paper policy was wrong. Nor did the evidence have any noticeable impact on the civil servants: they remained wedded to all-out expansion. Where it did have an impact was on the Opposition: parties in opposition are always more willing to consider alternatives. The Lib Dems early on came up with a sensible policy for limiting the growth of aviation. It was necessary to convert the Tories.

David Cameron asked John Gummer to set up a Quality of Life Commission, and I was included in the aviation subgroup, chaired by the former MP and London mayoral candidate, Steven Norris. John Stewart and Tim Johnson were also members, and so was Sally Cairns. The group made some radical recommendations to limit the growth in air travel, which were published, with a foreword by George Osborne, as a Conservative policy statement: *Greener Skies.*

Meanwhile, down at low profile Gatwick we were wondering whether the new Heathrow runway would be found impracticable, bringing us back into the battle. Instead the Government gradually gave Heathrow more importance, shifting the priority for the first new runway from Stansted to Heathrow. Gordon Brown, now Prime Minister, supported by British Airways and the CBI, argued that it was essential to the survival of London to maintain Heathrow as an international hub.

Heathrow and Stansted campaigners each engaged in battle. The Stansted group had abandoned their previous long-winded title of the North West Essex and East Hertfordshire Preservation Association, abbreviated to the equally unmemorable NWEEHPA, and rechristened themselves Stop Stansted Expansion (SSE). They succeeded in raising prodigious sums of money, and employed a professional campaign director, Carol Barbone. She was extremely competent and personable, put our amateur efforts to shame, and became a good friend.

The first task for SSE was to resist a planning application by BAA to raise the limit on the number of passengers allowed to use the airport from 25 million a year to 35 million. Unlike Stansted (and Heathrow), Gatwick has never had a passenger limit. GACC and the local councils have always been prepared - reluctantly - to accept expansion up to full use of the existing runway but have drawn the line in the sand (or rather, in the muddy clay) at one runway. In part that has been because we realised that we were unlikely to win a public inquiry on restricting the use of the runway. Moreover, as has been proved at Heathrow, even when a limit is fixed, as soon as it is reached it is raised.

The Stansted public inquiry took place in 2007. A master stroke by SSE was to call an Eskimo to give evidence on climate change. Not any old Eskimo, but no less than Aqqaluk Lynge, the leader of Greenland's human rights organisation the Inuit Circumpolar Council and expert member of United Nations Permanent Forum on Indigenous Issues. *'Climate change is not just a theory to us in the Arctic;'* he said, *'it is a stark and dangerous reality. Human-induced climate change is undermining the ecosystem upon which Inuit depend for their physical and cultural survival. You may say that the expansion of London Stansted Airport will play only a small part in increasing climate change but everyone can say that about almost everything they do. It is*

*an excuse for doing nothing. The result of that attitude would be
catastrophic. The serious consequences affecting my people today
will affect your people tomorrow.'*

The Inquiry Inspector, acting on Government instructions,
dismissed this passionate appeal on the grounds that climate
change was a national not a local issue.

That was just the first Stansted inquiry. The main inquiry
into a BAA application to build the second runway was scheduled
for 2008. It was kyboshed by the Competition Commission. This
group of tunnel-vision businessmen had given their view that it was
essential to build several new runways in the London area in order
to create excess capacity and make competition bite. The environment did not come into their remit, and they went about their task
in an incredibly cack-handed fashion. Forcing BAA to sell Stansted
meant that the second Stansted public inquiry got lost in a jungle of
legal challenges.

The Heathrow battle was a titanic struggle, both in the sense
of pertaining to giants and in the sense of being similar to the sink-
ing of an unsinkable ocean liner. The giant who led the campaign
was the indefatigable John Stewart: he has written it up in *Victory
Against All the Odds*.[92]

The Heathrow campaign was supported by many MPs of
all parties, and by local councils representing two million people. It relied far more on direct action than we at Gatwick ever
envisaged, starting with the week-long climate camp near
Heathrow on 2007. Fearing a mass break-in to the airport, BAA
sought a High Court injunction to stop members of HACAN and
AirportWatch going anywhere near Heathrow. As AirportWatch
included among its members not only GACC but also the RSPB
and the National Trust, the injunction would apparently have
banned around 6 million people from using the Piccadilly Line,
the M25, the M4 and platforms 6 and 7 at Paddington Station ....
indefinitely! The injunction was thrown out and the campaign

got a huge boost in the national press. Those attending the climate camp impressed everyone by their seriousness and responsibility.

A lively and intelligent group of young people, desperately concerned about the impact of aviation on climate change, formed 'Plane Stupid'. They carried out a number of stunts, of which the most dramatic was climbing onto the roof of the Houses of Parliament and unfurling banners while providing a running commentary to the press on their mobile phones.

For several weeks the Sunday Times carried front page stories, based on Freedom of Information requests, of how the Transport Department had worked with BAA to push forward the Heathrow runway plans. The FoI requests were lodged by a young MP, Justine Greening – later to become a short-lived Secretary of State for Transport. A dramatic Parliamentary debate to approve the new runway took place in January 2009. Two junior Ministers resigned, one Labour MP opposed to the runway was suspended for dancing around with the mace, and the Government only just scraped through.

The vigorous campaigns at Heathrow and Stansted persuaded the Tories to announce that they would veto any new runways at either airport. We needed to get Gatwick added to the list and sought help from Francis Maude who was by now a member of the Shadow Cabinet. He suggested to Theresa Villiers, the Shadow Transport Secretary, that she should invite GACC to put our case to her. Unfortunately her assistant got the initials muddled (not everyone knew that we had won the Battle of Acronym) and invited the Gatwick Airport Consultative Committee instead. They were chuffed to be invited, and told her that Gatwick was a very fine airport but that they could not comment on the runway issue!

We were, however, invited to rectify the situation by sending Theresa Villiers a one-page explanation of why a new runway should be ruled out. One of the key new points we made was that the apparent lack of agitation around Gatwick was deceptive: it was the result of there being no current threat. If there were to be a real threat, the strength of protest could be expected to be just as great as at Heathrow and Stansted. To support this hypothesis we gave the fact that there were more country lovers, members of CPRE, in Surrey, Sussex and Kent than in any other English county.

Francis Maude (whose heart was in the right place – his mother had been a leading member of CPRE) was in a key position: he was in charge of drafting the Tory manifesto. Having chaired the many meetings at Gravetye over the previous six years he understood the issues, and we reinforced the message by inviting him to address our GACC annual meeting in November 2009.

One promise from a key Cabinet, or Shadow Cabinet, Minister is worth any number of high profile demonstrations. There is a tendency among protesters to confuse razzmatazz with success. It is easy to believe that a demo by a few hundred people waving placards or wearing colourful T-shirts is going to change Government policy. Coverage in the local press and on local TV gives a warm glow. But government ministers don't read the local press or watch local TV.

By now Ferrovial had sold Gatwick to Global Infrastructure Partners. In an astute move the new owners appointed Sir David Rowlands, former Permanent Secretary at the Department for Transport, as chairman of the Gatwick Board. He knew his way round the corridors of power, and he certainly could tell which way the political wind was blowing. When he made his first public visit to Gatwick in January 2010, he announced that: 'a second runway will not be built in the foreseeable future.' And added for good measure: 'The simple fact is that we at Gatwick have not a shred of interest in a second runway.'

With our experience of past broken promises from politicians and civil servants, we took this with a good-sized pinch of salt, and waited for confirmation at the general election. The Conservatives went into the 2010 election with a promise to block any new runways in the South East. So did the Liberal Democrats. When the Coalition Government was formed on 12 May, the joint statement of policy included:

- **The cancellation of the third runway at Heathrow.**
- **The refusal of additional runways at Gatwick and Stansted.**

ROSEMARY COTTAGE

Sixty years on
1952 – 2012

Looking back over sixty years, how have Charlwood and the neighbouring towns and villages fared since Gatwick was first mooted as
a full-scale airport?

Aircraft noise was appalling and intolerable in the late 1960s
through to the 1980s but aircraft are now much quieter. Thanks to
constant pressure from environmental groups around the world,
the noisiest types of aircraft have been banned. At Gatwick the
amount of noise permitted at night has been progressively reduced.
The noise contours showing the areas affected by serious noise have
shrunk dramatically. Thousands of people in Horley and Crawley
no longer suffer acute noise.

Nevertheless aircraft are still annoying. Especially in summer when one wants to be in the garden, or to sleep with the
windows open. Noise travels further in warm weather, and in
summer there are more flights. Members of GACC, living under
flight paths up to 20 miles from the airport, still complain bitterly
of the constant disturbance.

With rising living standards has come a desire for a
better quality of life; expectations of peace and quiet have

risen. When Gatwick was closed for six days in April 2010, as a result of the ash spewed out by the unpronounceable Eyjafjalla-jökull volcano, the peace and quiet were palpable. So were the blue skies without a contrail in sight.

The Government state in their latest policy document that their aim is to 'limit and if possible reduce' the number of people affected by aircraft noise.[93] Good. But it is difficult to see how this aspiration can be reconciled with the admission by Gatwick Airport in the small print of its 2012 master plan that the planned growth in the number of flights will mean an increase in noise.

The biggest change in the past sixty years has probably been the road traffic, partly due to the proximity of the airport. In village centres cars and vans make more noise than the aircraft. Meeting neighbours and conversing in the street is no longer a pleasure. Danger is ever-present: young children can no longer be allowed out unattended and the old cannot cross the road without risking their lives.

After a number of fatal accidents in the 1980s, I chaired a group of local parish councils covering the area between Gatwick and Dorking – Charlwood, Newdigate, Capel, Leigh, Betchworth and Brockham. We requested road humps in each village. The County Council told us not to be silly: such an idea was impossible, but fifteen years later they proposed an ambitious traffic-calming scheme bearing a remarkable resemblance to our suggestions. Charlwood was picked as the first of the six villages to be calmed. A Government White Paper referred to it as a model to be emulated, but it caused uproar. Farmers blocked the road with their combine harvesters. Motorists swore at pedestrians. Pedestrians swore at motorists. At a public meeting everyone swore at each other. The County Council went ahead and installed artificial cobblestones to slow the traffic and emphasise the historic character of the village.

The experiment was a total failure. Motorists soon discovered that the faster they drove the weaker the vibrations. The cobblestones started to break up and were ignominiously removed.

Satnavs now direct even more speed-crazed glassy-eyed robots down our rural roads.

Some nearby villages such as Newdigate or Brockham are lucky: they have lots of cars parked along the road through the village centre, forcing traffic to slow to a safe speed. As the World Health Organisation has pointed out, pedestrians have a 90 per cent chance of survival if struck by a car travelling at under 20 miles per hour. But Charlwood suffers from the misfortune of a straight road with too few parked cars. Pedestrians have less than a 50 per cent chance of surviving an impact at 30 mph, and almost no chance of surviving at 50 mph.

Although the countryside has been preserved by strict planning and strict enforcement of the green belt rules, there have been big changes. We now have two farms instead of twenty. Intensive farming and road traffic have meant that we have lost our hares, hedgehogs and stoats while other friendly species, such as weasels, grass snakes, slow worms and butterflies have all suffered a sad decline. The filling-in of most ponds means we have few frogs, few newts and few dragonflies. But we still have badgers and moles; there are plenty of deer (which eat our roses and the flowers on the churchyard graves), foxes and grey squirrels. We have lost our lapwings and larks but buzzards have arrived in Edolphs Copse; we have barn owls, herons and woodpeckers, and a wide selection of garden birds providing good sport for the sparrowhawks.

All that would apply equally to almost any other village in the south east of England. But 'equally' - that is just the point. Our village has not suffered disproportionate damage.

Despite the proximity of the airport our community thrives. In 1968 the village suffered a severe flash flood and for a few days was cut off from the outside world. With the ground floors submerged there was nothing to do except go upstairs and make the best of it. Hence when a group of local thespians gathered to raise funds to repair the parish hall they called their play 'Love in the Fludde'. Love begat the Charlwood Players.

Thanks to the records of recent village history kept by Colin Gates, the Players have been able to write many of their own historical productions. One was the 1995 production of 'Bless 'em All', to commemorate the fiftieth anniversary of the end of the second world war. Forty actors, each with four costume changes, contributed to the Millennium celebrations. The need to raise funds for the new church loo saw the Players and the choir coming together to tell in emotive song, dance and drama the story of the church, as observed by the thousand-year-old yew tree that stands in the churchyard.

The Charlwood Society, founded in 1970, has taken a leading role in promoting pride in the village, holding exhibitions of village history and resisting a plethora of planning applications that would cumulatively have left the area looking like the environs of Heathrow. The Society was given a new lease of life by the creation in 2010 of the Charlwood History Group that has already attracted some 150 members. The Women's Institute has been reborn as a new group of fun-loving wine-drinking computer-literate young ladies. There is football on 'the Rec' every Saturday in winter, and cricket in summer. A new sports pavilion is planned by the parish council. A recent survey done as part of a slowly emerging parish plan showed that what people in Charlwood valued most was the sense of a friendly community, and living in a rural village set in the countryside.

The village appears to produce a range of musical talent from trumpet playing to Appalachian dulcimer strumming. The church choristers turn a dab hand to instrument playing. Two current residents have released albums that have reached the top of their respective genres. Traditional folk is enjoyed at a regular monthly pub session. The Big Band performs with some of the UK's top jazz professionals; there is a madrigal choir and a ladies clog dance team.

Alongside newcomers, old families with deep local roots remain. Just to give one example: in 1896 an Act of Parliament created parish councils: in Charlwood, Thomas Wickens, the village master builder, was appointed clerk to the new parish council. His son, also Thomas Wickens, inherited the building business and took over as parish clerk, holding the post until 1964. He was also the village undertaker, maker of coffins and – most conveniently – the registrar of births, marriages and deaths. His three daughters, Jean, Celeste and Marion, have always lived in the village. For many years Jean was the village historian, a mantle that has now passed to her son, John Shelley. And John, who lives in a medieval cottage (illustrated at the head of this chapter) which he has lovingly restored to its original condition, can trace his Charlwood ancestry, through his father's side of the family, back to the owners of Gatwick Manor in the 13th century.

Like every other village in England we have lost most of our shops. In the 1950's we had a butcher, a baker (but no candlestick maker), a cobbler, two drapers and three grocers, a fish shop, a sweet shop and a post office. But we still have three pubs, a village store, a café, a hairdresser, a kitchen design and equipment shop, a computer shop, and several builders.

As someone who had moved into the village remarked recently: 'We chose Charlwood because it has got everything that makes an ideal village – a good village school, good pubs, a good church, and lots going on.' He could have added that another thing that helps to make a village a village, not an amorphous suburb, is that we still have the church bells rung every Sunday and a rector living in The Rectory. A few years ago when the diocese wished, as in so many other English villages, to sell off 'The Old Rectory' as a desirable gentleman's residence, we soon scotched that plan.

Battles against the airport have given us practice in resisting threats to our rural idyll. An entertainment company planned to hold a mini-Glastonbury on Edolphs Farm with up to 60,000 people attending regular music festivals.   They booked a room at the Stanhill Court Hotel to tell the locals what fun it would be. Two hundred locals turned up in opposition mode, and told them loudly and firmly that it was not their idea of fun.   It emerged that the promoters had failed to contact the various landowners on whose land it was proposed to park cars and provide access to the site; and all the landowners refused permission. After an hour or two of noisy debate, the promoters retreated, saying that they had no idea that people felt so strongly about protecting the countryside.

The owners of Edolphs farm tried again with a similar licence application but in August 2012 that was refused by the council, after another impressive show of opposition by the battle-hardened people of Charlwood.

The threat of a new runway proved more long-lasting. The Coalition Government, elected in 2010, set about devising a new aviation policy. BAA and British Airways ran a frenetic lobbying campaign, plastering Westminster underground station with posters aimed at persuading Members of Parliament to support a third runway at Heathrow. The stakes were high: London's position as a world class capital was claimed to depend on having a hub airport capable of competing with Paris, Amsterdam or Frankfurt, all of which had four or more runways.

Boris Johnson, Mayor of London, whose equally eccentric and amusing father had been a colleague of mine in the 1960s, pressed for an airport in the Thames Estuary, similar to the Marinair proposals considered by RUCATSE. Alternative plans for a vast new airport on the Hoo peninsular, not dissimilar to the Cliffe plans rejected in 2003, were put forward by the architect, Sir Norman Foster. Almost every day for months the press contained speculation on where the new runways should be built.

Justine Greening, the anti-Heathrow runway Transport Secretary, was reshuffled, giving rise to much speculation that the Conservatives were preparing to support a third runway at Heathrow – or somewhere else. The Lib Dems, however, stuck to their environmental policy of opposing any new runway in the South East. Thus there was no way the Government could reach a decision without breaking up the coalition. To postpone the problem, and to apply a dose of rational reasoning (a process that had been noticeably missing), a Commission was set up, with Sir Howard Davies as chairman, to make recommendations on where to put new runways and whether a large hub airport is required - a remit remarkably similar to that of the Roskill Commission in 1968-71.

So, to mangle an omen, the tangled wings rumble on. No solution is in sight. Indeed it is a problem that has no solution: there is nowhere in South East England where a four runway airport can be built. We would today be looking at a very different situation if our suggestion in 1954 of Sheppey or Cliffe had been taken seriously. Or if Maplin had not been cancelled. Or if the airlines had not rubbished the plans for Marinair in 1993. But the world has moved on, and none of those options are acceptable.

It is the view of the great majority of scientists that climate change is real. Perhaps not in my lifetime but in the lives of my children and grandchildren, it will create huge floods, severe droughts, extermination of many species, mass starvation and mass migrations. Air travel will come to be seen as one of the main culprits. Since the British take more flights than any other major nation we have a moral responsibility to take a lead in encouraging the rest of the world that the growth in air travel must be constrained.

Meanwhile the threat of another runway at Gatwick remains. The end of the legal agreement in 2019 approaches. In October 2012 Sir David Rowlands, chairman of Gatwick Airport Ltd, he who had 'not a shred of interest in a new runway', announced that the airport would be studing options for a new runway. So it looks as if we may well face another battle, but it will be fought by a new and younger generation.

I do not, however, believe that any sane Government would resurrect the idea of a new runway to the north of Gatwick. That has been rejected six times, in 1953, in 1970, in 1985, in 1993, in 2003, and in 2010. Each of these six decisions has been taken by the Government of the day, by Churchill, Heath, Thatcher, Major, Blair and Cameron, after their expert advisers had undertaken detailed studies.

I trust that the British people would never permit the destruction of a whole lively village community, or the desolation of around eighty listed buildings – a worse destruction of our heritage than at any time since Hitler's blitz.

Nor do I believe that airline passengers would take warmly to landing or taking off through a hole in a hill.

As for a new runway to the south, the owners of Gatwick themselves admit that there is no space to build it other than comparatively close to the existing runway. It would leave little room for aircraft to manoeuvre around on the ground, and little room for them to snuggle up to the new terminal. I do not believe that the airlines would be over keen to use an airport where the aircraft would be constricted in their movements on the ground or where – to parade the same old omen again – they might get their wings tangled.

The truth is that Gatwick is just too small – like Northolt, Heston, Hendon, Fairoaks, Croydon, Redhill, Biggin Hill – all aerodromes which were famous in their day but which were abandoned, at any rate for large-scale international aviation, when it was found that they could never be expanded.

So Charlwood will survive. The old church will stand for another thousand years. The Saxon rebels may rest in their graves. I hope they feel that we put up a good fight on their behalf.

Some Charlwood and Gatwick dates

c. 1080	Charlwood church built
25 December 1170	Rector excommunicated by Archbishop Beckett
1241	Land in Charlwood assigned to John de Gatwyke
c. 1280	De Gatwyke aisle added to Charlwood church
c. 1300	Church murals painted
c. 1480	Chantry chapel (now the choir stalls) built
1846	Charlwood common enclosed
1891	Gatwick race course opened
Late 1920s	Field used for private flying
1 August 1930	Gatwick aerodrome licensed
6 June 1936	Beehive terminal opening ceremony
30 July 1952	Government states Gatwick to be Heathrow 'alternate'.
July 1953	'London's Airports' White Paper
16 March – 8 April 1954	Public Inquiry into development of Gatwick
17 January 1956	First meeting Gatwick Airport Consultative Committee
31 March 1956	Construction starts
9 June 1958	Enlarged Gatwick Airport opened
17 November 1970	Runway extension public inquiry opens
9 June 1978	Helicopter service to Heathrow introduced
14 August 1979	No new runway legal agreement signed
29 Jan – 11 July 1980	North Terminal public inquiry
June 1980	Charlwood Festival
18 March 1988	North Terminal opened
22 July 1993	RUCATSE report published.
27 February 2003	Consultation on Gatwick runway options
16 December 2003	Future of Air Transport White Paper
8 June 2006	BAA purchased by Ferrovial
3 December 2009	Gatwick purchased by Global Infrastructure Partners
17 October 2012	Study into Gatwick runway options announced

Index

Notes

1 British Economic Policy 1970-74. Institute of Economic Affairs. 1975.
2 Published by The Conservative Research Department. 2009. Other contributors include Chris Patten, Michael Dobbs and David Cameron.
3 The Freemen of Charlwood. Ruth Sewill and Elizabeth Lane. 1951. Second edition with postscript by Brendon Sewill. 1980
4 www.british-caledonian.com
5 Councils and amenity/environmental groups who expressed support for the no runway legal agreement or which have been members of GACC. Some may no longer be in existence.
6 Viscount Swinton.
7 Gatwick: the Evolution of an Airport. John King. Sussex Industrial Archaeological Society. 1986
8 Flight. Popular Flying.
9 Golden Gatwick. John King and Geoff Tait. The Royal Aeronautical Society. 1980
10 For the full wartime record see http://www.gatwickaviationsociety.org.uk/history.asp
11 Four Centuries of Charlwood Houses. Joan Harding. The Charlwood Society. 1976
12 In 1951 the number of cars in the UK was 2 ¼ million
13 Census 1951 England and Wales. County Report for Surrey
14 Hansard. 1st March, 1949.
15 Gatwick: the Evolution of an Airport.
16 Sir David Rowlands became chairman of GAL when the airport was bought by Global Infrastructure Partners in 2009.
17 22 July 1952.
18 Published 7 October 1952
19 Parish Council Minutes 19 November 1952
20 Cabinet Papers. C.C. (52) 11 November 1952
21 Cabinet Papers. C.C. (53) 198. 17 July 1953
22 Cabinet Papers. C.C. (53) 44th Conclusions
23 London's Airports. Cmd 8902. 1953
24 Tragedy of Errors. Gatwick Press. October 1953
25 The T5 Inquiry ran from May 1995 to March 1999. The time from the planning application to the government decision was eight years.
26 The Times 23 July 1953
27 Report of an Inquiry into the Proposed Development of Gatwick Airport. Cmd 9215. July 1954.
28 Report of the Inquiry (above). Paragraph 279
29 Cabinet Papers. C.C. (54) 7 September 1954
30 Gatwick Airport. Cmd 9296. 1954
31 The only other one, to my knowledge, is Mumbai.
32 Bertram Carter of Bedford Square, London. Pupil of Edwin Lutyens.
33 Later Lord Balfour of Inchrye. 'Wings over Westminster' 1973, quoted in Heathrow, 2000 Years of History. Philip Sherwood. 2009
34 Daily Telegraph 18 February 1959.
35 Parish Council Minutes 29 March 1965
36 ANMAC. The Aircraft Noise Monitoring Committee.
37 The Stansted Affair. Olive Cook. 1967
38 Stansted Airport White Paper. May 1967
39 Roskill Report. Summary, paragraph 61.
40 The Times. 25 April 1970
41 Charlwood Society (Gatwick Airport Group). Minutes. May 1970
42 Cublington - A Blueprint for Resistance. David Perman. 1973
43 The Course of My Life. Edward Heath. 1998
44 Cabinet Paper. CP(71) 34. 27 March 1971.
45 Letter from the Department of the Environment to the British Airports Authority. 9 May 1972
46 Observer. 19 March 1973
47 Cabinet Memorandum. 12 July 1974. C(74) 73

[48] Department of the Environment Circular 8/71 'Local Government Reorganisation in England - Proposed New Areas.' 1971

[49] The Times. 6 December 1971

[50] The Times. 8 February 1974

[51] Heathrow News. February 1995.

[52] Later Sir Philip Otten, retired as a Judge of the Court of Appeal in 2001.

[53] This evidence and other Gatwick papers are held privately but it is hoped that they will be deposited in a new Charlwood archive room planned by the parish council.

[54] Minutes of Mason's Recreation Ground Charity 11 December 1981 and 25 January 1982

[55] Charlwood Parish News April 1982

[56] The Times 1 July 1988

[57] Surrey County Council Gipsy Subcommittee confidential report 13 February 1986

[58] Mole Valley District Council Minutes 10 October 1988

[59] Now Lord Baker of Dorking.

[60] Now Lord Howe of Aberavon

[61] Now the Aviation Environment Federation of which Tim Johnson is the Director

[62] The Airports Policy Consortium.

[63] Covell Matthews Partnership International

[64] Runway Capacity to Serve the South East. Report. Department of Transport. July 1993.

[65] The proposal would have raised the capacity of Gatwick to 80 million passengers a year, twice its full capacity with one runway but more than three times its actual use in 1993.

[66] This is not strictly accurate – Hilary was awarded an MBE for her 27 years on the Gatwick consultative committee.

[67] Campaigns of the Norman Conquest. Matthew Bennett. 2001.

[68] Quoted in The Norman Conquest. Marc Morris. 2012

[69] John of Worcester. c.1100- 1130

[70] Orderic Vitalis. 1075 – c. 1142

[71] Domesday Book: Surrey John Morris. 1975.

[72] Thomas Becket. Frank Barlow. 1986

[73] Dictionary of Saints. Penguin. 1965.

[74] Quoted in The Norman Conquest. Marc Morris. 2012

[75] May 1995 to March 1999.

[76] BAA plc Annual Report 2000/01

[77] Sunday Telegraph. 3 December 2006

[78] Section 127 (2) of the Telecommunications Act 2003: 'A person is guilty of an offence if, for the purpose of causing annoyance, inconvenience or needless anxiety to another, he .... persistently makes use of a public electronic communications network.'

[79] The Environmental Law Foundation put us in touch with solicitor Laura Higgs of Bindmans.

[80] Cabinet Minutes 25 March 1971 CM (71)

[81] www.airportwatch.org.uk

[82] The Future Development of Air Transport in the United Kingdom: South East. Department for Transport. July 2002.

[83] The Future Development of Air Transport in the United Kingdom: South East. Second edition. Department for Transport. February 2003.

[84] The Future of Air Transport. December 2003. Paragraph 11.83

[85] Interim Master Plan. October 2006

[86] The Contribution of the Aviation Industry to the UK Economy. Oxford Economic Forecasting. November 1999.

[87] Intergovernmental Panel on Climate Change. http://www.ipcc.ch/publications_and_data/publications_and_data_reports.shtml#1

[88] Special Report on Aviation and the Global Atmosphere. IPCC. 1999

[89] Predict and Decide: Aviation, climate change and UK policy. Sally Cairns and Carey Newson. Environmental Change Institute, University of Oxford. September 2006

[90] Fallible Forecasts. GACC. March 2008

[91] http://m.conservatives.com/News/News_stories/2007/03/Greener_skies.aspx

[92] http://hacan.org.uk/resources/reports/victory.pdf

[93] Air Transport White Paper 2003, repeated in the Draft Aviation Policy Framework 2012

[94] Gatwick master plan. July 2012. Paragraph 10.3.6